WATCH WITH

BY THE SAME AUTHOR

The Pastoral Care of the Mentally Ill (SPCK)
Pastoral Care in Hospitals (SPCK)
When Sickness Comes (Church in Wales)
Visiting Ours: A Layman's Guide to Hospital Visiting (Church in Wales)

WATCH WITH THE SICK

Compiled by
NORMAN AUTTON

LONDON
SPCK

First published as
A Manual of Prayers and Readings with the Sick 1970

SPCK
Holy Trinity Church
Marylebone Road
London NW1 4DU

Revised and enlarged edition
with new title
first published 1976

Printed in Great Britain by
Camelot Press Ltd., Southampton

ISBN 0 281 02924 5

CONTENTS

ACKNOWLEDGEMENTS

Thanks are due to the following for permission to reproduce material of which they are the publishers, authors, or copyright holders:

Edward Arnold (Publishers) Ltd
BBC Publications
Church in Wales Publications
The Church Pastoral Aid Society
The Churches' Council for Health and Healing
Wm. Collins Sons & Co. Ltd
The Dean of King's College, Cambridge
Miss Margaret Dewey
Evans Brothers Ltd on behalf of Rivingtons
The Faith Press Ltd
The Reverend A.S.T. Fisher
Forward Movement Publications
Mrs Elizabeth Goudge
The Guild of Health
The Guild of St Raphael
Miss Phoebe Hesketh
Longman Group Ltd
Lutterworth Press
Macmillan, London and Basingstoke, on behalf of Mrs Frances Temple
Mayhew-McCrimmon Ltd, Great Wakering, Essex
The Mothers' Union
A.R. Mowbray & Co. Ltd
John Murray (Publishers) Ltd
Oxford University Press
Mark Pearson Esq.
The Publications Committee of the Episcopal Church of Scotland
The Right Reverend the Bishop of Salisbury
S.C.M. Press Ltd
The Standing Committee of the General Synod of the Church of Ireland
The United Society for the Propagation of the Gospel
Mrs Jean Yeomans

The Authorized Version of the Bible and the Book of Common Prayer 1662 are Crown copyright; extracts used herein are by permission.

Extracts from the New English Bible, second edition © 1970, are used by permission of Oxford and Cambridge University Presses.

Extracts from the Prayer Book as proposed in 1928 are printed by permission of the Central Board of Finance of the Church of England; extracts from the Canadian Prayer Book are printed by permission of Cambridge University Press; extracts from *St Hugh's Prayer Book* are printed by permission of Mrs K. Durrant.

Material from *Alternative Services*, *Second Series*, Baptism and Confirmation, is printed by permission of the Registrars of the Convocations of Canterbury and York.

Prayer 103 is taken from *Epilogues and Prayers,* written and copyright © 1963 by William Barclay. Used by permission of S.C.M. Press and Abingdon Press.

Extracts from *Parish Prayers*, ed. Frank Colquhoun, appear by permission of Hodder & Stoughton Ltd and Morehouse-Barlow Co. Inc; extracts from *Prayers for Christian Healing,* ed. A.E. Campion, appear by permission of A.R. Mowbray & Co. Ltd and Morehouse-Barlow Co. Inc.

Prayers 74, 83, 86, 90, 99, and 146 are adapted from pp. 38, 79, 113, 120, 123, and 124 of *Prayers for Help and Healing* by William Barclay, copyright © 1968 by William Barclay. Reprinted by permission of Wm. Collins Sons & Co. Ltd and Harper & Row, Publishers, Inc.

Prayer 57 is taken from *More Prayers for the Plain Man* (American title *A Guide to Daily Prayer*) by William Barclay. Copyright © 1962 by William Barclay. Reprinted by permission of Wm. Collins Sons & Co. Ltd and Harper & Row, Publishers, Inc.

While every effort has been made to trace the owners of copyrights, this has not been possible in a number of cases. We apologise most sincerely for any infringement of copyright or failure to acknowledge original sources and shall be glad to include any necessary corrections in reprints of this book.

PREFACE

It is hoped that this revised and enlarged collection of offices, prayers, and readings will prove a handy pocket-book for use with the sick either at home or in hospital. New prayers have been added since the earlier edition in 1970, some of which are familiar, others have been adapted for use, and a few have been specially compiled. They are meant to provide material and direction for prayer and to be freely adapted, rather than to be lavishly or rigidly followed. Some can be learnt by heart or used as models for extempore prayer, for there is a world of difference between merely reading prayers and praying. For the sake of uniformity all the selected readings from the New Testament are from the New English Bible, but those who use the manual will be free to choose other versions, should they feel that they speak more helpfully in certain individual circumstances. So, too, the language of the prayers can be adapted in the same way. Notes have been appended to certain sections to give guidance to those who are beginning their ministry to the sick.

Easter 1975 NORMAN AUTTON

Jesus, I have to watch people suffering,
and there seems so little that I can do to help.
Lord, show me what to do and what to say.
Take my very helplessness and in some way
use it to help the suffering. Your mother and your
beloved disciple who watched by you when
you were dying knew the pain of being utterly
useless when someone they loved was dying.
Lord, give me the kind of strengthening
compassion which they had and which can make
suffering less lonely and more bearable.
And, Lord, ease the pain of those whom I watch with
by giving them a sense of your strengthening presence.

(*Michael Hollings and Etta Gullick*)

General Instructions

PRAYING WITH THE SICK

Pray as if everything depended on God and
act as if everything depended on oneself.
(St Ignatius of Loyola)

Prayers with the sick have no preconceived pattern, for the priest will attempt, as far as is possible, to meet the varied needs of each individual patient. The ministry of prayer will therefore be flexible and free. Sometimes it may be helpful to use extempore prayer; at other times well-known prayers, tested and tried through centuries, speak to the patient's condition by their very familiarity. At all times, however, the priest's prayers must be as his Lord's – short and simple, perhaps beginning with the Lord's Prayer recited slowly and distinctly, and ending with the Blessing (cf. 1 Peter 3.9). There will be occasions when he will stand at the bedside; more often he will sit alongside the patient. Whatever the method used or manner adopted, the priest's prayers with the sick should always be 'in the name of Jesus Christ', for then 'Jesus assumes the responsibility and all the consequences. He steps forward for us, steps into the place of the person praying' (Kierkegaard). They will seek their fulfilment 'through Jesus Christ our Lord'.

1. Praying with the sick seems more personal and penetrating than praying for the sick. Wherever it is known, the Christian name of the patient may be used: 'Simon, Simon. . . I have prayed that your faith may not fail' (Luke 22.31); 'Jesus asked him, "What is your name?"' (Mark 5.9: cf. Rom. 1.9; Eph. 1.15, 16). Sick people often experience a deep sense of loneliness and frustration: 'Sir. . . I have no one. . .' (John 5.7), 'Why this waste?' (Matt. 26.8), when prayer becomes increasingly difficult, particularly with the onset of pain or weakness, and such personal prayer goes a long way to symbolize true sympathy and identification.

2. Prayers with the sick should be full of the presence and power of God. Brother Lawrence confesses that all his prayers and the whole of his prayers added up to 'nothing else but a sense of the presence of God'. We shall be meeting together with him about the sickness of another. Like the four friends of the Gospel story

(Mark 2.1–5) we shall lay his needs at the feet of our Lord, leaving them there in perfect confidence and trust.

3. Prayers with the sick will be positive. Bartimaeus in his blindness prayed, 'I want my sight back' (Mark 10.51); the leper prayed, 'Sir, if only you will, you can cleanse me' (Matt. 8.2). Neither made mention of his complaint. Mary and Martha brought the illness of their brother, Lazarus, to our Lord with the words, 'Sir, you should know that your friend lies ill' (John 11.3). The recitation of medical case histories was deemed unnecessary. 'I have heard a man offer a prayer for a sick person', wrote C.S. Lewis, 'which really amounted to a diagnosis followed by advice as to how God should treat the person' (*Letters to Malcolm: Chiefly on Prayer*). Positive prayers will nevertheless include whatever resentment or bitterness the patient may feel, for it must be shown that these too can be offered to God. Fr Raymond Raynes C.R. in one of his letters to a friend in hospital writes: 'Of course talk with our Lord about it all in your own way and do what the Psalmist says, "Complain unto the Lord". Ask questions, provided you allow our Lord to answer them.'

Those who pray will therefore see the patient strong and well in body, mind, and spirit. 'I tell you, then, whatever you ask for in prayer, believe that you have received it and it will be yours' (Mark 11.24). So often we expect too little, such is our lack of faith. It is not so much whether Christ will heal but rather how he will heal.

4. Prayers with the sick will be persistent. 'He spoke to them. . . that they should keep on praying and never lose heart' (Luke 18.1: cf. 11.9). Brief acts and petitions can be frequently repeated. In that fifteenth-century classic, *The Cloud of Unknowing*, the unknown author has a chapter on 'Short Prayer Pierceth Heaven', in which he says of prayer: 'If they are in words. . . then they are very few words; the fewer the better. If it is a little word of one syllable, I think it better than if it is of two or more, in accordance with the work of the spirit.' He quaintly tells us that a very short word 'pierces the ears of Almighty God more quickly than any long psalm, churned out unthinkingly'.

Jesus prayed in the Garden of Gethsemane 'using the same words as before' (Matt. 26.44). We must not lose patience nor expect quick and easy results. No true prayer is ever lost. 'I knew already that thou always hearest me' (John 11.42). St Augustine reminds us that even when God refuses the desire of our hearts he never refuses the heart of our desire.

5. Praying with the sick will be costly. If our prayers are to mean anything to God, they must mean something to ourselves. 'The fruitful prayer is the prayer with a drop of blood in it' (Le Plus). Sometimes requests for intercessory prayer are made rather light-heartedly without realizing what is really involved. Intercessions that cost little will avail little. 'I am, often, I believe, praying for others when I should be doing things for them. It's so much easier to pray for a bore than to go and see him' (C.S. Lewis). 'Clots of blood' (Luke 22.42) fell at Gethsemane.

Each intercessor should be prepared to say, 'for his (her) sake I now consecrate myself' (cf. John 17.19). In our intercessory prayers we shall not only think of what God can do but also what we ourselves should do, for he will not do for us what he can only do through us. Prayers without deeds will be as songs without words. We must be prepared to be used and often at a greater cost than perhaps we like. 'Here am I, send me' (Isa. 8.5). 'The things, good Lord, that I pray for, give me grace to labour for' (St Thomas More). It was Mahatma Gandhi who said that God comes to a starving man in the form of bread, and William Booth, founder of the Salvation Army, once declared, 'Soup, soap and salvation belong together!' Our prayers with the sick will therefore be a supplement to, rather than a substitute for, personal action (cf. Jas. 2.14–17). They will be something more than passive contemplation; they will also involve active participation. Indeed, in their highest form they will be true identification. Only if we are prepared for them to be this can we truthfully be fellow-workers with Christ, for the cost of intercessory prayer is our share in the cost of redemption.

6. Prayers with the sick will be purposeful. 'Do you want to recover?' (John 5.6) – for full recovery is the process of developing Christ's life within ourselves. If we seek his glory then he will glorify himself in us. Healing must never be seen as an end in itself. Rather it is a means to an end – a greater glorification of Christ. We are healed to serve.

7. Prayers with the sick will include periods of stillness. 'Speak, Lord, for thy servant heareth' is a petition which can so easily be reversed. Silent prayer and meditation at the bedside will instil calmness and courage. 'In quietness and confidence shall be your strength.' 'Thou wilt keep him in perfect peace whose mind is stayed on thee.' The priest in the sickroom must take pains to see that such a mode of prayer is a period of living silence and not mere dead stillness.

8. Prayers with the sick will be full of praise and thanksgiving so that attention will be directed more to God than to ourselves. 'It is certain that whatever seeming calamity happens to you, if you thank and praise God for it, you turn it into a blessing' (William Law). Brother Lawrence, encouraging us to develop the art of practising the Presence of God, comments: 'He requires no great matters of us; a little remembrance of him from time to time, a little adoration. . . sometimes to offer him our sufferings, and sometimes to return him thanks for the favours he has given you and still gives you, in the midst of your troubles. . . Lift up your heart to him. . . you need not cry very loud: he is nearer to us than we are aware of.'

9. Prayers with the sick will require much personal preparation. We cannot pray effectively for others unless we ourselves are open and receptive channels of God's healing grace. The contagion of our own personal wholeness will speak much louder than the words of our prayers. 'The glory which thou gavest me I have given to them. . .' (John 17.22). Before the Kingdom can be brought to others it must first be deeply rooted within ourselves. Intercessory prayers should be the fruit of our intercessory lives.

10. Finally, all prayers with the sick should be linked with those of:

(a) *The People of God*. They should be seen in the context of the whole Church, the community of intercessors of which the hospital or sickroom and its staff are part. 'He will continue to deliver us, if you will co-operate by praying for us. Then, with so many people praying for our deliverance, there will be many to give thanks on our behalf for the gracious favour God has shown towards us' (2 Cor. 1.11). In our intercessory prayers we shall, too, be 'with angels and archangels and all the company of heaven'.

(b) *The Passion of Christ*. Our prayers form part of those of the Great Intercessor, for he 'is always living to plead on their behalf' (Heb. 7.25). At the heart of all our intercessions is the cross, on which he, the sinless one, suffered for each one of us. 'Not what I will, but what thou wilt' (Matt. 26.39) will mean that in our intercessions we are not trying to mould God's will to our own. C.S. Lewis used to underline 'done' in 'Thy will be done' to remind himself that he must be the active agent, to ask God to give him 'the same mind which was also in Christ'. Such a prayer may well include suffering and pain, but we can offer our sufferings to him in union with his (cf. Phil. 3.10). It means too that we can suffer joyfully for love of him, for each of us can say: 'This is my way of helping to complete, in my poor human flesh, the full tale of Christ's afflictions still to be endured, for the sake of his body which is the church' (Col. 1.24).

READING WITH THE SICK

When you read God's word, you must constantly be saying to yourself, 'It is talking to me, and about me'. (*Søren Kierkegaard*)

1. The passages of scripture which will be read at the bedside will speak of prayer and of penitence, of hope and of healing, of praise and of thanksgiving. They should be read slowly, intelligently, and meaningfully, making each selection relate to the patient's condition. 'Did we not feel our hearts on fire as he talked with us. . . and explained the scriptures to us?' (Luke 24.32).

2. As well as speaking we shall be listening; listening to Christ speaking through the pages of the Gospels. In this way we shall be holding, as it were, a dialogue with Christ. It is only then that his word becomes 'a lantern unto our feet and a light unto our paths' (Ps. 119.105).

3. Reading, like prayer, is a call to action. Suppose we are reading such a passage as Jas. 5.14–16 which tells of the healing ministry of the Church through prayer and sacrament. Enlightening as this is, it will avail us little unless we are prepared to co-operate with its teaching; unless 'the elders of the congregation' are praying; unless the sacrament of Holy Unction is being administered or instruction being given about its use. Both priest and patient must be ready to act upon each truth it reveals.

4. Discretion will be exercised over the use of various translations. For the older patient the more familiar language of the Authorized Version will probably mean more than the modern phrases of present-day versions. However, it is important that whatever is read and heard will be seen not as a dead language of the past but as a living voice of the present; its message being as relevant today as when it was first delivered. We shall so read that the patient will see as well as hear the Gospel.

5. With reading will go interpretation and instruction. 'How can I understand unless someone will give me the clue?' (Acts 8.31). 'Every inspired scripture has its use for teaching the truth. . .' (2 Tim. 3.16). Such teaching will be a test of our own knowledge

of the Bible through prayer, meditation, and recital of the Daily Office.

6. Members of the hospital and/or congregation will take their part in reading with the sick, particularly with the lonely, bed-ridden, and housebound, thus expressing the concern of the whole Church, the Body of Christ.

7. Unfortunately, it cannot be assumed that all patients will be 'familiar with the sacred writings which have power to make you wise and lead you to salvation through faith in Christ Jesus' (2 Tim. 3.15). Selections from various anthologies of prose and poetry such as *A Book of Comfort* by Elizabeth Goudge, or any of those listed on pp. 109–10, might be used with much profit to supplement the readings.

8. It will be helpful to leave with the patient a single sentence or phrase which sums up the contents of the selected passage which has been read. This can be used as an 'affirmation' or 'ejaculatory prayer' (see pp. 98–102) during a sleepless night, in pain, or before an operation.

9. Bibles and copies of the Gospels should be readily available on the ward or in the sickroom for the use of the sick, so that they can 'read, mark, learn' passages of their own choice. Gideon Bibles are particularly helpful and are normally available either on the bedside locker or in the hospital ward. They list appropriate passages to be used 'when afraid, anxious, depressed, discouraged, etc.'

10. The selected passage should be carefully studied by the reader in preparation for his visit, so that it will become so much part of the pastoral call 'that faith is awakened by the message, and the message that awakens it comes through the word of Christ' (Rom. 10.17).

INSTRUCTION WITH THE SICK

> I wish you could convince yourself that God is often nearer to us, and more effectually present with us, in sickness than in health. (*Brother Lawrence*)

Patients will obviously vary greatly in their understanding of the Christian faith. For those who have been familiar with the sacraments prior to their illness in hospital or at home there will be little need for further instruction before their administration. There will, however, be many who have a connection with the Church yet are unfamiliar with, for example, the laying on of hands and Holy Unction. Some will be entirely ignorant of the basic tenets of the Christian faith. To each patient, therefore, the priest will minister according to his particular needs.

Sickness can often be a unique opportunity for instruction provided the patient is not too weak, is ready and co-operative, and the teaching brief, simple, and straightforward.

First and foremost it will be necessary to create a meaningful relationship with the patient, gaining his full confidence and trust, and forming an opinion about his spiritual and mental state, supplementing this with as much information as he might have about his physical condition and the prognosis of his illness.

When this has been achieved the way may be open for instruction. One of the major practical difficulties will be the very limited opportunities at the priest's disposal, for the majority of patients are in hospital for a comparatively short period. It is therefore essential that more and more teaching be given in the parish.[1]

As far as is practical in the allotted time and in the present condition of the patient, the priest will attempt to:

1. build up full confidence in and co-operation with the doctors,

[1] Much help can be gained here through membership of the Guild of St Raphael, (Secretary: Revd D.G. Hollands), 14 Glenfield Road, Banstead, Surrey (Tel. Burgh Heath 53938) or the Guild of Health, Edward Wilson House, 26 Queen Anne Street, London W1M 9LB (Tel. 01-580 2492). The Churches' Council for Health and Healing, St Peter's Vestry, Hobart Place, London, SW1W OHH (Tel. 01-235 3305) may also be of help.

nurses, and all who will be ministering to the patient's needs;

2. establish a full understanding of the realization of the love of God and of the healing ministry;
3. further an appreciation of how suffering can be offered in patience and fortitude in union with Christ's all-sufficient sacrifices, and how evil can be transfigured through the victory of the cross;
4. instil faith and expectancy without raising false hopes;
5. help with prayer and meditation if the patient is well enough, and administer the sacraments;
6. encourage hope and deepen penitence;
7. prepare for a dignified and Christian death when the opportunity presents itself;
8. convey to the patient that he is being supported by the prayers and faith of the congregation in both hospital and parish;
9. see that his own ministrations are but part of the wider healing ministry of the whole Church;
10. exercise the utmost wisdom, discretion, and patience in all his dealings with his sick people.

For further details of instruction with different types of patient in various stages of their illness, suggestions for helpful literature available for the priest and the patient, and practical information concerning the administration of sacraments with the sick, see *Pastoral Care in Hospitals* (S.P.C.K. 1968).

For patients receiving their Holy Communion in hospital the following cards are available: 'Communion of the Sick', S.P.C.K. T3249; 'Communion of the Sick, Second Series', S.P.C.K. T3258.

THE LAYING ON OF HANDS AND HOLY UNCTION

> I cannot go to cure the body of my patient, but I forget my profession, and call unto God for his soul.
> (*Sir Thomas Browne*)

The sacramental act of the laying on of hands may be used either *(a) informally*: After explanation of its use with the patient and brief prayer, the priest will lay both hands firmly but gently upon the head of the patient, saying a prayer such as the following: 'May the grace of the Lord Jesus flow through you for the healing of soul, mind, and body, upon whom we now lay hands in his most holy name', and the blessing. Although used informally in this way the act should always be carried out with the utmost dignity and reverence; or *(b) formally* as an Office, for which the priest will carefully prepare the patient by acts of faith, penitence, prayer, and meditation. The present Office will be found rather lengthy and tiring by very sick persons, and the priest will use his discretion as to its abbreviation and be flexible about its official form. Whenever possible it will be made a corporate act, with the family, a few of the prayer group, or members of the hospital staff present, upholding both priest and patient in prayer.

The laying on of hands will sometimes lead up to and serve as a preparation for the sacrament of Holy Unction or be used in conjunction with it. The doctor and nursing staff should be informed about its administration to the patient, and have its full meaning and significance for healing explained, so that their own understanding, co-operation, and prayers will be forthcoming.

It will have been pointed out in preparation that the primary use of the laying on of hands is not for mere physical healing but rather that by simple faith and surrender to Christ he will express his own wholeness in and through the patient concerned. After administering the laying on of hands the priest will quietly leave the bedside, the patient trusting in the mercy and good will of the healing Christ and firmly believing that his healing power is working within him.

Preparation for Holy Unction will be similar to that already outlined for the laying on of hands – faith, repentance, and prayer. It cannot be overemphasized that the patient should have a clear understanding of the sacrament and a sincere desire for its use. Again, it is essential that the doctor's active co-operation be gained.

A small table will be available in the sickroom and placed at the bedside, prepared similarly as for Holy Communion, with which Holy Unction can be combined. On the white cloth will be placed the stock containing the hallowed oil, together with some cotton wool in a glass bowl. The oil will have been blessed by the Bishop for use (traditionally each Maundy Thursday) but the priest may do this himself before the anointing if necessary. He will dip his thumb in the holy oil, and anoint the patient on the forehead in the form of a cross, saying, 'N., I anoint thee with holy oil. . .' (see Office, p.34). The priest will afterwards wipe the patient's forehead with the cotton wool and also cleanse his own thumb and fingers. The cotton wool will be burnt after use.

Whereas the laying on of hands can be used frequently, Holy Unction is administered more sparingly and is usually reserved for those leading a sacramental life and for such periods as before an operation, long-drawn-out illness or weakness, acute pain, and emergencies. It is not to be mistaken for Extreme Unction, although obviously it can be used *in extremis* when occasion arises. It is the Church's great healing sacrament and much grace and blessing follow its administration. We shall be satisfied to leave the form of healing in the hands of God for it is not ours either to direct, dictate, or demand. Rather in faith the patient will be content to respond firmly and convincingly with others who have sought Christ's help in affliction: '"Do you believe that I have the power to do what you want?" "Yes, sir", they said. Then he touched their eyes, and said, "As you have believed, so let it be"' (Matt. 9.28–9).

Before and After Visiting

PRAYERS BEFORE VISITING THE SICK

O Lord, renew our spirits and draw our hearts unto thyself, that our work may not be to us a burden, but a delight; and give us such a mighty love to thee as may sweeten our obedience. O let us not serve thee with the spirit of bondage as slaves, but with cheerfulness and gladness, delighting ourselves in thee and rejoicing in thy work. (1)

We beseech thee, O Lord, to enlighten our minds and to strengthen our wills, that we may know what we ought to do, and be enabled to do it, through the grace of thy most Holy Spirit, and for the merits of thy Son, Jesus Christ our Lord. (2)

I will conceive of God to-day
    In Jesus as he heals men
        in body and soul.
I will stand by him as he restores them
    and see with what gentleness
        with what confidence
        with what searching love
God and man are made one. (3)

You know, O Lord, the duties that lie before me, the dangers that may confront me, the sins that most beset me. Guide me, strengthen me, protect me. (4)

All through this day, O Lord, let me touch the lives of others for good, by the power of your Holy Spirit, whether through the word I speak, the prayer I breathe, or the life I live. In the name of Jesus. (5)

Take, O Lord, my hands and use them, take my lips and speak through them, take my eyes and smile through them, take my heart and mind and will and use them all as lamps of love, by which your light may shine in all the darkness of this suffering world. (6)

O Lord, fit me for your use, and use me in your service. (7)

PRAYERS AFTER VISITING

We praise thee, O God, for all the blessings given to the sick for whom we have prayed. We thank thee for those who have been made whole, for those who are better, and for those who have been drawn closer to thee. We bless thee for the sense of thy presence enabling those who suffer to endure with patience. And finally we thank thee for bringing good out of evil, joy out of suffering, and above all for the cross of thy Christ and the certain hope of the redemption of body and soul to everlasting life. (8)

O Lord our God, into thy hands we commit all for whom we have prayed. Thou art infinite Love, infinite Wisdom, infinite Power. Bless them according to their several necessities out of the abundance of thy grace; through Jesus Christ our Lord. (9)

O Lord, forgive, we pray thee, what we have been; sanctify what we are; and order what we shall be. What we know not, teach us; what we have not got, give us; what we are not, make us; for Jesus Christ's sake. (10)

O Jesus, Master Carpenter of Nazareth, who on the cross through wood and nails didst work man's whole salvation, wield well thy tools in this thy workshop; that we who come to thee rough hewn may by thy hand be fashioned to a truer beauty and a greater usefulness; for the honour of thy holy name. (11)

SUITABLE READINGS BEFORE VISITING THE SICK

He now called the Twelve together and gave them power and authority to overcome all the devils and to cure diseases, and sent them to proclaim the kingdom of God and to heal. (Luke. 9.1–2)

He went round the whole of Galilee, teaching in the synagogues, preaching the gospel of the Kingdom, and curing whatever illness or infirmity there was among the people. His fame reached the whole of Syria; and sufferers from every kind of illness, racked with pain, possessed by devils, epileptic, or paralysed, were all brought to him, and he cured them. (Matt. 4.23–4)

Come to me, all whose work is hard, whose load is heavy; and I will give you relief. Bend your necks to my yoke, and learn from me, for I am gentle and humble-hearted; and your souls will find relief. For my yoke is good to bear, my load is light.

(Matt. 11.28–30)

The spirit of the Lord is upon me because he has anointed me;
He has sent me to announce good news to the poor,
to proclaim release for prisoners and recovery of sight for the blind;
to let the broken victims go free,
to proclaim the year of the Lord's favour. (Luke 4.18–19)

The Sacraments

PRAYERS BEFORE TAKING HOLY COMMUNION TO THE SICK

O Lord Jesus Christ, who hast provided for us Thy unworthy servants Thy holy and life-giving Sacrament; grant, I beseech Thee, to Thy priests, whom Thou dost call to consecrate these holy Mysteries, such purity and holiness of life that, through Thy mercies, they may be worthy to minister at Thy altars here, and to stand among Thy redeemed hereafter in Thy Kingdom. (12)

Cleanse the thoughts of our hearts, O Lord, as we come to partake of thy holy Sacrament; and enlighten our minds by thy Holy Spirit, that we may be delivered from all insincerity, from satisfaction with ourselves, and from failure to see how great is our need of thy grace. This we ask for thy dear Name's sake. (13)

We beseech thee, O Lord, to strengthen and confirm all communicants, and to lift them up more and more continually to heavenly desires; through Jesus Christ our Lord. (14)

O Lord, hear my prayer for all who intend to receive thy most blessed sacrament. Give them the help of thy spirit, that they may draw near in a warm faith, and with humble hearts may greet thee, O Lord our Saviour. (15)

Most gracious God, incline thy merciful ears to our prayers, and enlighten our hearts with the grace of the Holy Spirit, that we may worthily approach thy holy mysteries and love thee with an everlasting love. (16)

Come, Holy Ghost, and enlighten the minds of thy servants, that they may by faith discern the Lord's Body and Blood in the holy sacrament, to the great comfort and health of their souls, and the setting forth of the worship of thy great love and power and glory. (17)

PRAYERS AFTER TAKING HOLY COMMUNION TO THE SICK

Strengthen, O Lord, the hands which have been held out to receive Thy holy things; grant that they may be worthy of all that has been said and sung to Thy praise within Thy sanctuary, and may ever serve Thee. Grant that the tongues, which have uttered Thy praises may speak the truth, and that we who have received the living Body and Blood of Jesus Christ may be restored in newness of life: through the same Thy Son Jesus Christ our Lord. (18)

Defend, O Lord, thy children with thy heavenly grace, that they may continue thine for ever, and daily increase in thy Holy Spirit more and more, until they come unto thy everlasting kingdom. (19)

Remember, O Lord, what thou hast wrought in us, and not what we deserve, and as thou hast called us to thy service, make us worthy of our calling, through Jesus Christ our Lord. (20)

O God, who in a wonderful sacrament hast left us a memorial of thy passion, grant us, we beseech thee, so to venerate the sacred mysteries of thy body and blood that we may ever perceive within ourselves the fruit of thy redemption, who livest and reignest with the Father in the unity of the Holy Spirit, one God, world without end. (21)

Go before us, O Lord, in all our doings, with thy most gracious favour, and further us with thy continual help, that in all our works begun, continued, and ended in thee, we may glorify thy holy name, and finally by thy mercy obtain everlasting life. (22)

O praise God in His holiness: praise Him in the firmament of His power.
Praise Him in His noble acts: praise Him according to His excellent greatness.
Let everything that hath breath: praise the Lord. (23)

SUITABLE READINGS FOR HOLY COMMUNION

Whoever eats my flesh and drinks my blood possesses eternal life and I will raise him up on the last day. My flesh is real food; my blood is real drink. Whoever eats my flesh and drinks my blood dwells continually in me and I dwell in him. (John 6.54–6)

During supper Jesus took bread, and having said the blessing he broke it and gave it to the disciples with the words: 'Take this and eat; this is my body.' Then he took a cup, and having offered thanks to God, he gave it to them with the words: 'Drink from it, all of you. For this is my blood, the blood of the covenant, shed for many for the forgiveness of sins.' (Matt. 26.26–8)

When we bless the 'cup of blessing', is it not a means of sharing in the blood of Christ? When we break the bread, is it not a means of sharing in the body of Christ? Because there is one loaf, we, many as we are, are one body; for it is one loaf of which we all partake. (1 Cor. 10.16–17)

. . . every time you eat this bread and drink the cup, you proclaim the death of the Lord, until he comes.

It follows that anyone who eats the bread or drinks the cup of the Lord unworthily will be guilty of desecrating the body and blood of the Lord. A man must test himself before eating his share of the bread and drinking from the cup. (1 Cor. 11.26–8)

PRAYERS BEFORE ADMINISTERING HOLY BAPTISM

Almighty God, our heavenly Father, who in every generation dost bestow new sons and daughters upon thy Church; Grant that *these infants* may be born anew of water and of the Holy Spirit; that, daily increasing in the knowledge and love of thee, *they* may be numbered among the children of thine adoption; through

Jesus Christ our Lord, who liveth and reigneth with thee and the Holy Spirit, one God, world without end. (24)

O God, by Whose Spirit the whole body of the Church is multiplied and governed: preserve in the new-born *children* of Thy family the fullness of Thy grace; that, being renewed in body and soul, *they* may be fervent in the unity of the faith, and be counted worthy, O Lord, to serve Thee; through Jesus Christ our Lord. (25)

Almighty God, who at the baptism of thy Christ in the river Jordan didst declare him to be thine only-begotten Son: grant that in baptism *these* thy *servants* may be made his *members* by thy Holy Spirit, and become thy *children* in the family of the Church; through the same thy Son Jesus Christ our Lord, who with thee and the same Spirit is alive and reigns, one God, world without end. (26)

Heavenly Father, grant that by thy Holy Spirit *these children* may be born again and brought to know thee in the family of thy Church; that in newness of life *they* may overcome evil and grow in grace unto *their* life's end; through Jesus Christ our Lord. (27)

O Lord God, our heavenly Father, remember for good, we beseech thee, those who at this time are preparing for holy baptism. Strengthen their faith, enlighten their minds, purify their hearts; and grant that, by the washing of regeneration and renewal in the Holy Spirit, they may receive the fullness of thy grace, and ever remain in the number of thy faithful and elect children; through Jesus Christ our Lord. (28)

(Much will depend upon the urgency of the situation: often there will not be time for more than the actual words of the Baptism.)

The Blessing of the Water

Bless, we pray thee, this water, that all who are baptized in it may be born again in Christ; that being baptized into his death, and receiving forgiveness of all their sins, they may know the power of his resurrection, and may walk in newness of life.

The Baptism

The priest shall then take the child, and having asked his *name, shall dip* him *in the water, or pour water upon* him, *saying*:

N., I baptize you in the Name of the Father, and of the Son, and of the Holy Spirit. Amen.

The Signing with the Cross

The priest shall make a cross upon the forehead of the child, saying:

I sign you with the sign ✠ of the cross,

(*and here the People shall join with him, saying*)

to show that you must not be ashamed to confess the faith of Christ crucified, and manfully to fight under his banner against sin, the world and the devil, and to continue Christ's faithful soldier and servant unto your life's end.

Suitable Prayers where opportunity occurs (see pp. 28, 73–4)

PRAYERS AFTER ADMINISTERING HOLY BAPTISM

We thank thee, O Father, that by thy Holy Spirit thou hast caused *these persons* to be born again, to become thine own by adoption, and members of thy Church. And we pray thee, O Father, that, filled by thy spirit, *they* may live and grow in thy service and attain thy promises; through Jesus Christ our Lord. (29)

Grant that *they* may grow in the faith in which *they* have been baptized; grant that *they themselves* may profess it when *they* come to be confirmed; and grant that all things belonging to the Spirit may live and grow in *them*; through Jesus Christ our Lord. (30)

Bless, we pray thee, the parents of *these children*; give them the spirit of wisdom and love, that their home may be an image of thy eternal kingdom; through Jesus Christ our Lord. (31)

Almighty God, our heavenly Father, Who hast given unto us the Sacrament of Holy Baptism that souls thereby being born again may be heirs of everlasting salvation: we yield Thee hearty thanks for this Thy gift, and humbly we beseech Thee to grant that we who have thus been made partakers of the death of Thy Son may also be partakers of His Resurrection; through the same Jesus Christ, our Lord. (32)

Almighty God our heavenly Father, whose dearly beloved Son Jesus Christ shared with the Blessed Virgin Mary and Saint Joseph the life of an earthly home at Nazareth: Bless we beseech thee the home of *this child*; and give such grace and wisdom to all who have the care of *him*, that by their word and good example *he* may learn truly to know and love thee; through the same thy Son Jesus Christ our Saviour. (33)

God has received you by Baptism into his Church. We therefore welcome you into the Lord's family,

as fellow-members of the Body of Christ,
as children of the same heavenly Father,
as inheritors with us of the Kingdom of God. (34)

SUITABLE READINGS FOR HOLY BAPTISM

They brought children for him to touch: The disciples rebuked them, but when Jesus saw this he was indignant, and said to them, 'Let the children come to me; do not try to stop them; for the kingdom of God belongs to such as these. I tell you, whoever does not accept the kingdom of God like a child will never enter it.' And he put his arms round them, laid his hands upon them, and blessed them. (Mark 10.13–16)

I baptize you with water; but there is one to come who is mightier than I. . . . He will baptize you with the Holy Spirit and with fire. (Luke 3.16)

. . . Christ is like a single body with its many limbs and organs which, many as they are, together make up one body. For indeed we were all brought into one body by baptism, in the one Spirit, whether we are Jews or Greeks, whether slaves or free men, and that one Holy Spirit was poured out for all of us to drink.
(1 Cor. 12.12–13)

But the harvest of the Spirit is love, joy, peace, patience, kindness, goodness, fidelity, gentleness, and self-control. There is no law dealing with such things as these. And those who belong to Christ Jesus have crucified the lower nature with its passions and desires. If the Spirit is the source of our life, let the Spirit also direct our course. (Gal. 5.22–5)

PRAYERS BEFORE HEARING CONFESSIONS

O God, Who wouldest not the death of a sinner, but that he should be converted and live, forgive the sins of him who turns to Thee with all his heart, and grant him the grace of eternal life; through Jesus Christ our Lord. (35)

O God, our Judge and Saviour, set before us the vision of thy purity and let us see our sins in the light of thy holiness. Pierce our self-contentment with the shafts of thy burning love, and let love consume in us all that hinders us from perfect service of thy cause; for thy holiness is our judgement, so are thy wounds our salvation. (36)

O God, give me wisdom that I may judge the people according to right. Make me gentle and at the same time faithful. Enlighten me to advise wisely in difficult cases; suffer me not to be harmed or influenced by the evil I hear, and grant that in seeking to save others I may not fail of salvation myself; through Jesus Christ our Lord. (37)

O Lord, who has taught us that all our doings without charity are nothing worth: send thy Holy Ghost, and pour into our hearts that most excellent gift of charity, the very bond of peace and all virtues, without which whosoever liveth is counted dead before thee: grant this for thine only Son Jesus Christ's sake. (38)

FORMS OF ABSOLUTION

Our Lord Jesus Christ, who hath left power to his Church to absolve all sinners who truly repent and believe in him, of his great mercy forgive thee thine offences; and by his authority committed to me, I absolve thee ✠ from all thy sins, In the name of the Father, and of the Son, and of the Holy Ghost. Amen. (39)

Almighty God have mercy upon you, pardon and deliver you from all your sins, confirm and strengthen you in all goodness, and keep you in life eternal; through Jesus Christ our Lord. (40)

Almighty God, our heavenly Father, who of his great mercy hath promised forgiveness of sins to all them that with hearty repentance and true faith turn unto him: have mercy upon you; pardon and deliver you from all your sins; confirm and strengthen you in all goodness; and bring you to everlasting life; through Jesus Christ our Lord. (41)

PRAYERS AFTER HEARING CONFESSIONS

Father of all mercies, teach us to be merciful, as thou art merciful.

Father of all forgiveness, help us to forgive others, as thou hast forgiven us; knowing that, with what measure we mete, it shall be measured to us again; for Jesus Christ's sake. (42)

Now unto Him that is able to keep us from falling, and to present us faultless before the Presence of His glory with exceeding joy, to the only wise God our Saviour, be glory and majesty, dominion and power, both now and ever. (43)

O Lord Jesus Christ, accept this service, and whatever I may have done carelessly or amiss in this ministry of reconciliation, in thy goodness ratify and correct, that no harm to others may ensue through my negligence. I now commit to thy love all and each who have confessed to me. (44)

SUITABLE READINGS BEFORE AND AFTER HEARING CONFESSIONS

For if you forgive others the wrongs they have done, your heavenly Father will also forgive you; but if you do not forgive others, then the wrongs you have done will not be forgiven by your Father. (Matt. 6.14–15)

. . . and when they reached the place called The Skull, they crucified him there, and the criminals with him, one on his right and the other on his left. Jesus said, 'Father, forgive them; they do not know what they are doing.' (Luke 23.33–4)

Jesus repeated, 'Peace be with you!', and said, 'As the Father sent me, so I send you.' Then he breathed on them, saying, 'Receive the Holy Spirit! If you forgive any man's sins, they stand forgiven; if you pronounce them unforgiven, unforgiven they remain.' (John 20.21–3)

Then Peter came up and asked him, 'Lord, how often am I to forgive my brother if he goes on wronging me? As many as seven times?' Jesus replied, 'I do not say seven times; I say seventy times seven.' (Matt. 18.21–2)

PRAYERS BEFORE ADMINISTERING THE LAYING ON OF HANDS AND HOLY UNCTION

Lord, increase our faith; and grant that we may have a clear vision of Thee in Thy healing power. Lay upon us the hands of Thy love. Teach us Thy compassion. Give us the confidence that can joyfully leave all our cares and diseases to the infinite power of Thy goodwill. We ask it, O loving Lord, for Thy mercy's sake. (45)

O Lord Jesus Christ, in obedience to thy command I
anoint with oil }
lay hands on } thy servant in thy name.
Grant that the prayer of faith may save *him*, and whatever sins *he* may have committed, let them be forgiven *him*, that whether in health or sickness, in life or death, *he* may praise and love thee for ever. (46)

O Almighty God, giver of life and health, who hast taught us in thy holy Word to pray over the sick, and to anoint them with oil in the name of the Lord, grant, we beseech thee, to this person, whom we anoint in thy name, refreshment of spirit, and, if it be thy will, perfect restoration to health; through Jesus Christ our Lord. (47)

O Almighty God, whose blessed Son did lay his hands upon the sick and heal them, grant, we beseech thee, to this person, upon whom we now lay our hands in his name, refreshment of spirit and, if it be thy holy will, perfect restoration to health; through the same thy Son, Jesus Christ our Lord. (48)

In the name of God most high we stretch forth the healing hands of God upon N. May release from pain be given *him*, and may *he* be restored to health of body, mind and soul; in the name of the Father, the Son, and the Holy Spirit. (49)

THE ANOINTING AND THE LAYING ON OF HANDS

The Bishop (or priest) shall say:

Hear what our Lord Jesus Christ saith: And these signs shall follow them that believe. In thy name they shall lay hands on the sick, and they shall recover. (Mark 16.17, 18)

R. The prayer of faith shall save the sick, and the Lord shall raise him up.

V. Lord, hear our prayer;

R. And let our cry come unto thee.

Then, the Bishop (or priest), laying his hands upon the sick person's head, shall say:

O Almighty God, who art the giver of all health, and the aid of them that look to thee for succour, we call upon thee for thy help and goodness mercifully to be shown upon this thy servant, that *he* may be healed of *his* infirmities and may give thanks unto thee in thy holy Church; through Jesus Christ our Lord. Amen.

The Bishop (or priest), dipping the thumb of his right hand in the holy oil, shall anoint the sick person on the brow, in the form of a cross, saying thus:

N., in the name of our Lord Jesus Christ I anoint thee with this holy oil, that thou mayest receive the anointing of the Holy Spirit, unto the healing of all thy infirmities of soul, and mind, and body. Amen.

Then, once more laying both his hands upon the sick person's head, he shall say:

As with this visible oil thy body is outwardly anointed, so may our heavenly Father grant of his infinite goodness that thy soul may inwardly be anointed with the Holy Ghost, and be filled with strength and comfort. May the Almighty God restore to thee (bodily) health and strength to serve him. May he send to thee freedom from all thy pains, troubles and diseases, whether of body or mind. May he pardon all thy sins and offences; and grant thee strength to serve him truly; that aided by his Holy Spirit, thou mayest have perfect victory and triumph over Satan, sin, disease, and death; through Jesus Christ our Lord, who by his death hath destroyed death, and now with the Father and the Holy Spirit evermore liveth and reigneth, God, world without end. Amen.

Or, if there be small hope of recovery, the following may be used:

May the Almighty Father who by the glorious Resurrection of his son, Jesus Christ, hath opened the Kingdom of Heaven to all believers, vouchsafe to anoint thee with his life-giving Spirit; and, if it be his will to call thee to himself, give thee triumph over sin and death, and bring thee to everlasting life; through the same Jesus Christ our Lord. Amen.

Here shall follow the Blessing in this form:

The Almighty God, who is a most strong tower to all them that put their trust in him, to whom all things in heaven, in earth, and under the earth, do bow and obey, be now and evermore thy defence, and make thee know and feel that there is none other name under heaven given to man, in whom and through whom thou mayest receive health and salvation, but only the name of our Lord Jesus Christ. Amen.

The peace of God, which passeth all understanding, keep your hearts and minds in the knowledge and love of God, and of his Son Jesus Christ our Lord: and the blessing of God Almighty, the Father, the Son, and the Holy Ghost, be amongst you and remain with you always. Amen.

The oil should be removed from the forehead of the sick person with a fragment of fabric or wool; and this should be burnt. The Bishop (or priest) (and the congregation) shall depart silently. It is here to be noted that if the person to be anointed seems to be at the point of death, Holy Communion should, according to ancient tradition, be administered after (not before) Holy Unction.

For other Forms see *A Diocesan Service Book*, edited and ordered by L.S. Hunter O.U.P. 1965. See also the Forms available from the Guild of Health and the Guild of St Raphael.

SUITABLE READINGS FOR THE LAYING ON OF HANDS AND HOLY UNCTION

. . . he summoned the Twelve and sent them out in pairs on a mission. He gave them authority over unclean spirits. . . So they set out and called publicly for repentance. They drove out many devils, and many sick people they anointed with oil and cured.

(Mark 6.7, 12–13)

Faith will bring with it these miracles: believers will cast out devils in thy name and speak in strange tongues; . . . and the sick on whom they lay their hands will recover. (Mark 16.17–18)

Is one of you ill? He should send for the elders of the congregation to pray over him and anoint him with oil in the name of the Lord. The prayer offered in faith will save the sick man, the Lord will raise him from his bed, and any sins he may have committed will be forgiven. Therefore confess your sins to one another, and pray for one another, and then you will be healed. A good man's prayer is powerful and effective. (Jas. 5.14–16)

May God himself, the God of peace, make you holy in every part, and keep you sound in spirit, soul, and body, without fault when our Lord Jesus Christ comes. He who calls you is to be trusted; he will do it. (1 Thess. 5.23–4)

EMERGENCY FORMS FOR ADMINISTRATION OF THE SACRAMENTS

Baptism

N., I baptize thee in the name of the Father, and of the Son, and of the Holy Ghost. Amen.

Absolution

N., I absolve thee from all thy sins in the name of the Father, and of the Son, and of the Holy Ghost. Amen.

Holy Communion

The Body of Christ.
The Blood of Christ.

Holy Unction

By this holy anointing may the Lord forgive thee whatever thou hast done amiss. Amen.

Spiritual Communion

Forms of Spiritual Communion will be found in the various books of Devotion. A most helpful booklet is *Spiritual Communion* by the Rt Revd J.T. Hughes, Bishop of Croydon, published by the Mothers' Union.

Prayers for General Use

THE MINISTRY OF HEALING

O God, the source of all health: so fill our hearts with faith in thy love, that with calm expectancy we may make room for thy power to possess us, and gracefully accept thy healing; through Jesus Christ our Lord. (50)

O God, the Creator and Father of all men, we praise thee that thy will is life and health and strength. Help all who are ill or in pain to place themselves in thy hands in loving trust, so that thy healing life may flow into them to make them well and strong, able and ready to do thy holy will; through him who has made known to us both thy love and thy will, even Jesus Christ our Lord. (51)

We come together, Lord, to pray for healing. We know each one of us needs to be made whole, to be renewed in your Spirit. And we ask for this. Send your Spirit on us. But we pray most especially and beg your strength and healing hand on N. and N. who are sick. Heal them: fill them with life and joy and peace in your love. (52)

THE HEALING CHURCH

O Lord and Master, Jesus Christ, who has borne our griefs and carried the burden of our infirmities; renew by your Holy Spirit in the Church, your gracious gifts of healing. Send forth your disciples again to preach the Gospel, to cure the sick and to relieve thy suffering children, to the glory of God the Father. (53)

Bless, O Lord, we beseech thee, all efforts of thy Church to fulfil its ministry to the bodies and souls of men. Give guidance and power to those who engage in this task, that neither sin nor suffering may separate men from thy love, and that thy healing grace may, through sacrament and prayer, be available to all thy children, so that many may know the blessing of thy word, 'Thy faith hath made thee whole'; who ever liveth and reigneth God, world without end. (54)

Almighty God, Who didst inspire Thy servant Saint Luke the physician to set forth in the Gospel the love and healing power of Thy Son: manifest in Thy Church the like power and love, to the healing of our bodies and our souls; through the same Jesus Christ our Lord. (55)

Grant, we beseech Thee, O merciful God, to all who minister healing and comfort to the sick and suffering Thy protection in the way of duty, strength and patience, tenderness and love for men, and that they may faithfully serve Thee in their office for the love of Thee; through Jesus Christ our Lord. (56)

SUDDEN CALAMITY

O God, I remember before you those on whom at this time disaster has come:

Bless those whose dear ones have been killed, and those whose dear ones lost their lives in seeking to save the lives of others.

Bless those who have lost their homes, those who have seen all that they toiled for a lifetime to build up lost in an hour.

Help us always to remember those whose job it is to risk their lives to rescue others or to keep them safe – those in the fire service, in the police service, in the medical service.

We shall forget this disaster, but we ask you always to remember those who will never forget, because life for them can never again be the same.

This we ask for your love's sake. (57)

PERSONAL RELATIONSHIPS

O God, help us to look at other people with new eyes because we have seen you revealed in Jesus Christ. May we recognize all men and women as your children, each one unique and each one loved by you. We believe that every relationship we make is grounded in your love; help us to act out the consequences of this belief and to let you work in us; for Christ's sake. (58)

THE HOSPITAL CHAPEL

Go with us, Lord, as we enter into thy holy house; and go with us, as we return to take up the common duties of life. In worship and in work alike let us know thy presence near us; till work itself be worship, and our every thought be to thy praise; through Jesus Christ our Saviour. (59)

MEETINGS OF HOSPITAL CHAPLAINS

O God our Father, of whose holy mysteries we are the ministers and stewards, direct us, we beseech thee, in all our doings with thy most gracious favour, enlighten us by thy Holy Spirit, as we consider together the opportunities and responsibilities of the Church in hospital in these times. Inspire our minds, assist our wills, and strengthen our hands, that we may not falter or fail in the work we have been given to do. (60)

DEDICATION OF A HOSPITAL CHAPEL

See *Order of United Service for the Dedication of a Hospital Chapel,* published for the Hospital Chaplaincies Council by the Church Information Office, Church House, Westminster, SW1P 3NZ.

DEDICATION OF A HOSPITAL UNIT

Almighty and Everliving God from whom cometh every good and perfect gift, be pleased to accept the thought, the gifts, the skills and labours which have made possible the building and equipping of this hospital unit. According to thy merciful purpose use, we beseech thee, the service of its doctors, surgeons, and nurses (and the work of research that will go forward here) for the health and wholeness of many people: through Jesus Christ our Lord. (61)

MEDICAL SCHOOL

Almighty God, who made man in thine own image, and called him to be a fellow-worker in thy eternal purpose, bless all who teach and all those who study in the medical school of our hospital. Grant to them insight and ingenuity in discovery, integrity and skill in the use of their knowledge and their powers, and at all times strength of mind and body for the constant demands of their high calling. (62)

SCHOOL OF NURSING

Almighty Father, grant that our School of Nursing may be a house of faith and fruitful study; and that our students may so learn truth as to bear its light along all their ways, and so learn Christ as to be found in him; who lives and reigns with thee and the Holy Spirit, one God, world without end. (63)

THOSE SITTING EXAMINATIONS

O God, who knowest the secrets of the heart, be with those who are now sitting examinations. Help them to face their task with calmness, confidence, and courage; with wisdom, faithfulness, and honesty; that they may do justice both to themselves and to their teachers, and set forth thy glory, who thyself art wisdom and truth, the giver of knowledge and of every virtue and good gift, in Jesus Christ our Lord. (64)

MEETINGS OF HOSPITAL COMMITTEES

O Lord and heavenly Father, who hast called us to serve thee in the administration of this hospital, and hast committed to us a solemn trust: prosper, we beseech thee, the work of our hands, and accept the service we now seek to render. Give us understanding of thy will in all matters that lie before us, and also grace faithfully to discharge our duties; that in all things we may seek the true well-being of those who are in our care. (65)

VISITORS

O Lord God, whose will and joy it is that thy children love one another: Bless our friendships, that they may be made happy and kept pure by thine unseen presence, now and at all times; through Jesus Christ our Lord. (66)

O heavenly Father, who hast bestowed upon us the comfort of earthly friends, bless all those who will be visiting patients in our hospital this day. Grant that their time together may be hallowed by thy presence, so that all our earthly love may be gathered up into the love of God, and thy kingdom made manifest to men in the homes of thy people. (67)

LEAGUE OF FRIENDS

O Lord Jesus Christ, bless the work of the League of Friends of this hospital; increase in them daily that holy friendship, and bind us ever more closely to one another in our concern for the needs of our patients and in our common love of thee. (68)

Prayers for the Staff

HOSPITAL AND STAFF

O Christ, Great Healer, who wills that men should be whole in body, mind and spirit: Fill the hearts of doctors and nurses everywhere with your power and your love so that they may be true instruments of your will. Grant them the knowledge that for all men the seeking of your kingdom first, in utter committal to you, is the way to wholeness; for your name's sake. (69)

Almighty Lord God, bless this hospital and all who are in it. May those who come here sick or injured, or needing an operation, learn something more of thee while they are within these walls, and under thy blessing be restored to health and strength. Give them comfort and courage in time of pain, and patience to wait on thee, knowing that all things work together for good to them that love thee; through Jesus Christ our Lord. (70)

O Lord God, who dost dispense thy healing power through the service of doctors and nurses and all who tend the sick, grant to these thy servants wisdom and skill, sympathy and patience; and send thy blessing on all who labour to prevent suffering and to forward thy purposes of love; through Jesus Christ our Lord. (71)

O Lord Jesus Christ, who in thy life on earth didst heal both the souls and the bodies of men: guide, we pray thee, all who now minister to body or to soul, and grant that those who serve things spiritual may not despise the body, nor those who treat the body set at nought the soul; but that, patiently seeking to understand the unity of our human nature, they may work together for the cure of all sickness and disease, and for the recovery of all that true health which is thy gift to those who wait upon thee. (72)

O Lord Jesus Christ, who hast said that, inasmuch as we do it unto one of the least of these Thy brethren, we do it unto Thee: look upon Thy servants who are called to nurse the sick and suffering children. Give them patience and fortitude, wisdom and love, and the grace and guidance of Thy Holy Spirit; that they may faithfully minister to those to whom Thou shalt send them, and be found worthy at the last to receive Thy eternal reward. (73)

SURGEONS, PHYSICIANS, AND PSYCHIATRISTS

O God,
When people come to
Surgeons, Physicians and Psychiatrists,
help them always
to ease the pain
and to strengthen the weakness of their bodies
and to calm the anxieties of their minds.
Help them never to think of them as cases,
but always as persons.
Help them to remember that,
when they bring health to the sick and the suffering,
the healing work of Jesus
is being continued through them,
and that they are helping you
to defeat the world's disease and pain. (74)

O merciful Father, who hast wonderfully fashioned man in thine own image and hast made his body to be a temple of the Holy Ghost: sanctify, we pray thee, all those whom thou hast called to study and practise the arts of healing the sick, and the prevention of disease and pain. Strengthen them in body and soul, and bless their work, that they may themselves live as members and servants of Christ, and give comfort to those whom he lived and died to save; through him who now liveth with thee in the unity of the Holy Ghost, one God, world without end. (75)

O God, guide the hands of thy servants, the surgeons of this hospital, and use them for thy service, giving them gentleness and skill. Grant them wisdom and strength that as a result of their endeavours they may deliver many from disease and pain. Let thy hand bless both them and all who come under their care. (76)

O God of Love, we pray for our psychiatric hospitals and for the doctors and nurses in their work of mercy and healing. Bless the mentally sick, especially those known to us, whom we remember in our hearts before thee. . . . Do for them whatever is for their good, and comfort them with thy presence, through Jesus Christ our Lord. (77)

NURSING STAFF

O Lord the healer of all our diseases, bless all whom thou hast called to be sharers in thine own work of healing, with health alike of body and soul; that they may learn their art in dependence upon thee, and exercise it always under thy sanction and to thy glory; who livest and reignest with the Father and the Holy Ghost, one God, world without end. (78)

O Lord, let thy perpetual providence guide and direct the conduct of our hospital, that doctors and nurses alike, together with the patients committed to our care, may be brought through contact with the mystery of suffering into union with thee, where alone it is solved. (79)

NIGHT STAFF

Let your presence, O God, refresh and strengthen those who have watched through the night on behalf of others, in sickroom and in hospital, and give them your peace; through Jesus Christ our Lord. (80)

Jesus, our Lord, keep watch with those who nurse through the dark hours, that in the light of thy presence they may see clearly what thou wouldst have them do. Let thy blessing be upon all who serve while the world sleeps, and bring them safely through the darkness to the coming day. (81)

OVERSEAS STAFF

O God, who hast made of one blood all nations upon the earth, and called all mankind thy children, bless, we beseech thee, all doctors, nurses, and students from overseas who serve in the hospitals of our land. Help us to labour together with them in fellowship and mutual understanding and concern. (82)

ADMINISTRATORS

O God,
Help those engaged in administration to remember
  that in their own way
  they too are engaged in the work of healing.
Help them to remember that
  behind every record card and letter
  there is a living person with a living need.
Keep them from becoming the kind of administrators
  who are more interested
  in procedures and statistics
  than in persons and people.
Help them always to remember
  that ultimately they are dealing with human beings
    and keep them human. (83)

We ask thy blessing, O God, on all who work in and for this hospital, particularly the administrative staff, that they may all be inspired with the knowledge that they are carrying on the work of thy Son Jesus Christ in the healing of the sick and the relief of pain. Grant that they may always have this ideal of service before them, and set forward thy purposes for the welfare of mankind. (84)

O Lord God Almighty, guide we pray thee, all those to whom thou hast committed the administration of this hospital, and grant to them special gifts of wisdom and understanding, of counsel and strength, that upholding what is right and following what is true, they may obey thy holy will and fulfil thy divine purpose; through Jesus Christ our Lord. (85)

BEFORE VISITING THOSE WHO MOURN

Lord, teach me what to say when I go to visit those who have just been bereaved. I feel utterly powerless in the face of their grief. They have to suffer so much. I am distressed for them, but words seem to fail me. Act through me, and make me the instrument of your comfort even if I say very little. Give me understanding compassion and give them faith in your strength, and peace so as to be able to endure their pain and loneliness which is so very deep. O Help of the helpless, help us all in our distress for the sake of your Son who knew the depths of human suffering.

(203)

THOSE ENGAGED IN THE SOCIAL SERVICES

O God,
You have given Social Workers a very important place
  in the life and work of this hospital.
Give them
  patience
    with those who are foolish and helpless
    and disorganised and even ungrateful.
Give them
  sympathy
    with those who are lonely and old
    with those who are anxious,
    with those who are worried.
Help them
  to see things clearly
  and to take decisions quickly and firmly,
And help them at all times
  to desire only to help and comfort. (86)

Almighty God, whose compassions fail not, and who hast taught us to have compassion upon those in need, prosper, we pray thee, the work of our welfare agencies. Stir up the wills of all our people to support them in the relief of want and suffering, and let us not rest until we have provided for the needs of thy children, giving generously as thou hast given to us. (87)

O Lord, we pray that thou wilt hasten the time when no man shall live in contentment while he knows that his neighbour has need. Inspire in us and in all men the consciousness that we are not our own but thine and our neighbours', for his sake, who prayed that we might all be one in him, Christ Jesus our Lord. (88)

O God, our heavenly Father, who knowest our needs and dost care for us all, we pray for all social workers, who by their skill and training help to relieve the fears and anxieties of those who are troubled. Bless and strengthen them in thy service, that they may be compassionate in their care of patients and their families, and so help to promote health and well-being; for the sake of Jesus Christ, our Lord. (89)

HOSPITAL CHAPLAINS

O God,
bless all hospital chaplains,
and all who come to visit people
  in hospitals and in infirmaries and in nursing-homes.
Give them sympathy
  so that they may really and truly enter
    into the anxieties and the fears and the pains
      of those they visit.
Give them cheerfulness,
  so that their visit
    may be like a ray of sunshine.
Give them insight
  so that they may know
    when to stay
    and when to go.
Help them never to visit just as a duty,
but to come because they really care
and really want to help. (90)

O Lord our heavenly Father, whose blessed Son came not to be ministered unto, but to minister, we beseech thee to bless all hospital chaplains who give themselves to the service both of the sick and those who tend them. Endue them with wisdom, patience, and courage, that being inspired by thy love they may worthily minister in thy name, for the sake of thy Son, our Saviour Jesus Christ. (91)

O Lord Jesus Christ, the Good Shepherd who laid down thy life for the sheep, give to hospital chaplains the grace they need to fulfil their charge. Fill them with love for the souls committed to their care; guide them by thy Holy Spirit in their undertakings, that all they do may be pleasing in thy sight. (92)

HOSPITAL CHURCH SISTERS

Almighty God, giver of all good things, who of thy divine providence hast appointed a diversity of ministrations in thy Church, mercifully behold thy servants who work as Hospital Church Sisters. So fill them with thy Holy Spirit that by both word and example they may faithfully and joyfully serve thee, in the hospitals of our land to the glory of thy name and the building up of thy Church; through Jesus Christ our Lord. (93)

Almighty God, we beseech thee to bless the work of Church Sisters who are serving with the Chaplains in many of our hospitals. With the help of thy grace may they so fully and faithfully minister to the needs of both the patients and staff, that by the dedication of their lives and the power of their prayers many may be made whole; through Jesus Christ our Lord. (94)

THOSE ENGAGED IN MEDICAL RESEARCH

O God, who declarest thy almighty power in showing mercy and pity and who revealest to men in each new discovery a part of thy truth; enable with thy grace, we pray thee, the dullness of our blinded sight, and grant a new vision to all those who serve thee in their search for the cause of cancer and its cure. Mercifully direct them in thy path of knowledge; grant them the realization that through thee all things are possible; pour upon them the abundance of thy inspiration, and finally lead them to victory, that the scourge of cancer may be ended, and that we, being freed from this burden of fear, may live continually in thy love and service. (95)

Eternal God, Creator and Lord of all things, you have given men minds and wills to discover the secrets of the universe: give vision and courage to those engaged in scientific work, that by their patient studies and research we may advance in our understanding of your purpose for the world, and be better able to serve the needs and welfare of mankind. (96)

Almighty God, of Whose only gift cometh insight and understanding: guide and prosper, we beseech Thee, those who labour in societies and associations devoted to scientific study and research, that through them knowledge may be increased and flourish; and grant that in Thy light they may see light, Who art the fountain of all wisdom; through Jesus Christ our Lord. (97)

Almighty God, who art the Father of truth and understanding, shed forth, we beseech thee, upon those engaged in medical and surgical research the light of thy heavenly guidance; grant to them the spirit of patient discernment, that they may be skilled to discover the way of health and healing; and strengthen them with the assurance that they are fellow-workers together with thee: through Jesus Christ our Lord. (98)

PORTERS, ORDERLIES, AND DOMESTIC WORKERS

O God, give to
Porters and Domestic Workers
pride in their work
And help them to do it gladly and cheerfully
so that they may bring sunshine and happiness
into the wards in which they work.
Help them always to remember
that they and their work
are essential to the healing of the patients
in this hospital. (99)

O Lord Jesus Christ, who in thy earthly life didst share man's toil, and hallow the labour of his hands, prosper all who maintain the domestic work of this hospital, and give them pride in their work, a just reward, and joy both in supplying need and in serving thee; who with the Father and the Holy Spirit livest and reignest, ever one God, world without end. (100)

ANXIOUS FAMILIES

Almighty, everlasting God, comfort of the sorrowful, and strength of the weary, may the prayers of all who call upon thee in any trouble, or those anxiously awaiting news of . . . come unto thy presence. Help us who minister to them, and so endow us with the grace of sympathy and compassion that we may bring to them both help and healing; through Jesus Christ our Lord. (101)

Prayers and Readings with Patients

THE SICK AND SUFFERING

Lord Jesus, who wast silent when men nailed thee to the cross, and by pain didst triumph over pain, pour thy Spirit, we beseech thee, on thy servants when they suffer, that in their quietness and courage thou mayest triumph again; who livest and reignest in the glory of the eternal Trinity, God world without end. (102)

Lord Jesus, when you were on earth, they brought the sick to you and you healed them all. Today we ask you to bless all those in sickness, in weakness and in pain. . . . Grant that we in our health and our strength may never find those who are weak and handicapped a nuisance, but grant that we may always do and give all that we can to help them and to make life easier for them. (103)

Almighty and Merciful God, Creator and Redeemer,
we bring before thee all who are sick in body, mind, or spirit.
Let them feel secure in thy love, and know that with thy grace all shall be well, in sickness or in health, in life or in death,
through Jesus Christ, our Lord. (104)

Almighty God, we commend all sufferers to thy loving care, especially those who come for healing here. Grant them patience in their distress; cheer and uphold them in mind and body, and grant that by their treatment and care here they may be restored to health and strength: through Jesus Christ our Lord. (105)

O Almighty and everlasting God, we praise thee for teaching us through the cross and resurrection of thy Son that suffering can be a creative force. Grant, we pray thee, that as his humiliation won glory and life, so the sufferings and endurance of those who follow him may be used to bring his presence and his power into a needy world, through the same Jesus Christ our Lord. (106)

O Lord we pray thee for all those who are weighed down with the mystery of suffering. Reveal thyself to them as the God of Love who thyself dost bear all our sufferings. Grant that they may know that suffering borne in fellowship with thee is not waste or frustration, but can be turned to goodness and blessing, something greater than if they had never suffered, through him who on the cross suffered rejection and hatred, loneliness and despair, agonizing pain and physical death, and rose victorious from the dead, conquering and to conquer, even Jesus Christ our Lord.
(107)

Merciful Father, help all who suffer pain of body or grief of heart, to find in you their help; and as Jesus suffered pain in his body and healed it in others, help them to find their peace in him, and by your mercy be renewed in strength of body and mind, through Jesus Christ our Lord. (108)

READINGS WITH THE SICK

And may the God of hope fill you with all joy and peace by your faith in him, until, by the power of the Holy Spirit, you overflow with hope. (Rom. 15.13)

The Lord is near; have no anxiety, but in everything make your requests known to God in prayer and petition with thanksgiving. Then the peace of God, which is beyond our utmost understanding, will keep guard over your hearts and your thoughts, in Christ Jesus.

And now, my friends, all that is true, all that is noble, all that is just and pure, all that is lovable and gracious, whatever is excellent and admirable – fill all your thoughts with these things.

The lessons I taught you, the tradition I have passed on, all that you heard me say or saw me do, put into practice; and the God of peace will be with you. (Phil. 4.6–9)

. . . God himself has said, 'I will never leave you or desert you'; and so we can take courage and say, 'The Lord is my helper, I will not fear; what can man do to me?' . . . Jesus Christ is the same yesterday, today, and for ever. (Heb. 13.5–6, 8)

Here is the proof that we dwell in him and he dwells in us: he has imparted his Spirit to us. Moreover, we have seen for ourselves, and we attest, that the Father sent the Son to be the saviour of the world, and if a man acknowledges that Jesus is the Son of God, God dwells in him and he dwells in God. Thus we have come to know and believe the love which God has for us.

(1 John 4.13–16)

Suitable Psalms

The Prayer Book version is suggested for older patients.

Revised editions can be used with others at the discretion of the priest.[1]

Ps.23 *The Lord is my shepherd*
Ps.27.1, 5–11, 13–14 *The Lord is my light...*
Ps.42.1, 5–8, 11 *Like as the hart desireth...*
Ps.62.1, 2, 7, 8 *My soul truly waiteth still...*
Ps.121 *I will lift up mine eyes unto the hills*

Healing Miracles

Mark 2.1–12 (The sick of the palsy)
Mark 5.22–43 (Jairus' daughter and the woman in the crowd)
Mark 6.7–13 (Healing ministry of the disciples)
Mark 10.46–52 (Blind Bartimaeus)
Luke 17.11–19 (Ten lepers)

[1] *The Revised Psalter Pointed*. C.U.P., Eyre & Spottiswoode, O.U.P., and S.P.C.K. 1966.
The Psalms: A New Translation. Fontana 1963.
Fifty Psalms: An attempt at a new translation. Burns & Oates 1968.
Also Revised Standard Version of the Bible, the Jerusalem Bible, the New English Bible, the Living Bible and Good News Bible.

THOSE NEWLY ADMITTED

The Almighty God, who is a most strong tower to all them that put their trust in him, to whom all things in heaven and earth do bow and obey, be now and ever more thy defence; and make thee know and feel, that there is none other name under heaven given to man, in whom and through whom thou mayest receive health and salvation, but only the name of our Lord Jesus Christ. (109)

Heavenly Father, whose Blessed Son our Lord took upon himself our infirmities and had compassion upon all sick and suffering folk; Hear our prayer for all who suffer in body or mind or spirit; and especially we pray for. . . Grant to them relief from pain, strength in their weakness, light in their darkness and, if it shall please thee, restoration to health. Enable them now to trust thee though thy way is hidden from their sight; and let them know that peace which is the gift of thy Holy Spirit. (110)

We pray thee, O heavenly Father, for all those who have just arrived in this our hospital and are not yet used to this manner of life; for those who are afraid, and especially for those waiting for an operation. O loving Shepherd, in thy great love and mercy give them confidence and peace, and faith to trust in thee. (111)

Lord, he whom thou lovest is sick, we need say no more and worry no more. Do for him according to his need – hold him with thy hand in thine unfailing love – him whom we love and whom thou lovest. (112)

Almighty, everlasting God, comfort of the sorrowful and strength of the weary, may the prayers of all that call upon thee in any trouble come into thy presence; that they may rejoice that in their necessity thy mercy has been with them; through Jesus Christ our Lord. (113)

O Lord and heavenly Father, who dost relieve those who suffer both in soul and body, stretch forth thine hand, we beseech thee, to heal the sick and ease their pain; that by thy mercy they may be restored to health of body and mind, and show forth their thankfulness in love to thee and service of their fellow men; through Jesus Christ our Lord. (114)

READINGS WITH PATIENTS NEWLY ADMITTED

Indeed anything you ask in my name I will do, so that the Father may be glorified in the Son. If you ask anything in my name I will do it.

If you love me you will obey my commands; and I will ask the Father, and he will give you another to be your Advocate, who will be with you for ever – the Spirit of truth. The world cannot receive him, because the world neither sees nor knows him; but you know him, because he dwells with you and is in you. I will not leave you bereft; I am coming back to you. (John 14.13–18)

Dwell in me, as I in you. . . . I am the vine and you the branches. He who dwells in me, as I dwell in him, bears much fruit; for apart from me you can do nothing.. . . As the Father has loved me, so I have loved you. (John 15.4, 5, 9)

Then what can separate us from the love of Christ? Can affliction or hardship? Can persecution, hunger, nakedness, peril, or the sword? . . . yet, in spite of all, overwhelming victory is ours through him who loved us. For I am convinced that there is nothing in death or life, in the realm of spirits or superhuman powers, in the world as it is or the world as it shall be, in the forces of the universe, in heights or depths – nothing in all creation that can separate us from the love of God in Christ Jesus our Lord. (Rom. 8.35, 37–9)

. . . take up God's armour; then you will be able to stand your ground when things are at their worst, to complete every task and still to stand. . . . Give yourselves wholly to prayer and entreaty; pray on every occasion in the power of the Spirit.

(Eph. 6.13, 18)

This letter is to assure you that you have eternal life. It is addressed to those who give their allegiance to the Son of God.

We can approach God with confidence for this reason: if we make requests which accord with his will he listens to us; and if we know that our requests are heard, we know also that the things we ask for are ours. (1 John 5.13–15)

THE ANXIOUS

Set free, O Lord, the souls of Thy servants from all restlessness and anxiety. Give us that peace and power which flow from Thee. Keep us in all perplexity and distress, that upheld by Thy strength and stayed on the rock of Thy faithfulness we may abide in Thee now and evermore. (115)

O God of peace, Who hast taught us that in returning and in rest we shall be saved, and in quietness and in confidence shall be our strength: by the might of Thy Spirit lift us, we pray Thee, to Thy presence, where we may be still and know that Thou art God; through Jesus Christ our Lord. (116)

Affirmations with the Anxious

Say to them that are anxious, 'Be strong, fear not'. (Isa. 35.4)

Fear nothing, for I am with you, be not afraid, for I am your God. I strengthen you. I help you. I support you with my victorious right hand. (Isa. 41.10)

I will fear no evil: for thou art with me. (Ps. 23.4)

I will say unto the Lord, Thou art my hope and my stronghold: my God, in him will I trust. (Ps. 91.2)

The Lord is my light and my salvation; whom then shall I fear. . .? (Ps. 27.1)

. . . though I am sometime afraid, yet put I my trust in thee. (Ps. 56.3)

. . . the angel said, 'Do not be afraid; I have good news for you: there is great joy coming to the whole people.' (Luke 2.10)

You are always with me, and everything I have is yours. (Luke 15.31)

Peace is my parting gift to you, my own peace, such as the world cannot give. Set your troubled hearts at rest, and banish your fears. (John 14.27)

There is no room for fear in love; perfect love banishes fear. (1 John 4.18)

O Lord, in thee have I trusted: let me never be confounded. (*Te Deum*)

WAITING FOR THE DOCTOR

Lord, give patience to those who are waiting to see the doctor. Stop them from feeling frustrated, angry or agitated about being late. Make them see that waiting affords an opportunity for turning to you, of praying to you for others or for themselves. Help them to realise that all time is in your hands, and that no time spent waiting with you is wasted. (117)

O Lord Jesus Christ, let the light both of thy pains and of thy triumphs shine upon thy servants in suffering and distress, to give them faith in thy good purpose, the support of thy presence, and strong confidence in thy power to heal and save; who art with the Father and the Holy Spirit God everlasting. (118)

O blessed Jesus, smooth away the cares from those who are anxious, and lead them into the paths of thy peace, where all their fears shall be lost in the brightness of thy love. (119)

SURGICAL PATIENTS

Father of compassion and mercy, who never failest to help and comfort those who cry to thee for succour, give strength and courage to this thy *son* in *his* hour of need. Hold thou *him* up and *he* shall be safe; enable *him* to feel that thou art near, and to know that underneath are the everlasting arms; and grant that, resting on thy protection, *he* may fear no evil, since thou art with *him*; through Jesus Christ our Lord. (120)

Bless thy servant, O Lord God, and grant to *him* the strength that is needful. Give the surgeons and nurses thy grace, that by their ministrations thy will may be accomplished in loving service. (121)

O loving Father, we commit N. with perfect trust into thy hands. Watch over *him* and protect *him* in the hour of weakness, and grant that when *he* becomes unconscious to earthly things *his* thoughts may be turned to thee. Bless and guide thy servants who shall tend *him* and give them good success; through Jesus Christ our Lord. (122)

Blessed Lord, comfort and strengthen thy servant, and deliver *him* from all fear of the unknown. Give *him* peace and courage and trust in thy divine will. May *his* operation restore *him* to health and strength, that *he* may live to praise thy goodness, and be better fitted to serve thee here below. This we ask for the sake of Jesus Christ our Lord. (123)

THOSE UNDERGOING TRANSPLANT SURGERY

O God, our heavenly Father, creator of our bodies and of all that exists; we thank you for the knowledge and skill of surgeons and doctors, and for the advances that have been made in combating disease. We pray that all those in the forefront of medical and surgical research may be guided both in the practical and ethical aspects of their work. May the good of the patients never be sacrificed for the sake of prestige or any other unworthy cause. May the side effects and complications induced by some new treatments be seen and overcome. May all be done in the spirit of him who went about healing all manner of sickness and disease among the people, your Son, Jesus Christ our Lord. (124)

MEDICAL PATIENTS

Almighty and eternal God, giver of life and health, grant that by thy goodness and mercy to this thy servant and to those who minister to *him he* may be restored to health and may in the body of thy Church walk before thee humbly and faithfully all *his* days; through Jesus Christ our Lord. (125)

O God who by the might of thy command canst drive away from men's bodies all sickness and infirmity, be present in thy goodness with this thy servant, that, *his* weakness being banished and *his* health restored, *he* may live to glorify thy holy name; through our Lord Jesus Christ. (126)

INVALIDS AND BEDRIDDEN

O most loving Father, who willest us to give thanks for all things, to dread nothing but the loss of thee, and to cast all our care on thee, who carest for us; preserve us from faithless fears and worldly anxieties, and grant that no clouds of this mortal life may hide from us the light of that love which is immortal, and which thou hast manifested unto us in thy Son, Jesus Christ our Lord. (127)

O Lord Jesus Christ, the help of the helpless and companion of the lonely: we ask you to bless all those who are unable to leave their homes or to join in public worship. Grant that they may always be confident of your presence with them, and of their oneness with the whole family of your church; and grant that with one mind and one voice we all may worship you O Christ who, with the Father and the Spirit, reigns for evermore. (128)

We pray thee, Lord, for all those who are in isolated places, or by infirmity are confined to home or hospital. Bless to them the word of the gospel over the air and on television, and grant to them a full and consoling sense of thy presence, that together with us they may be strengthened and uplifted by the gift of grace. (129)

We remember before thee, O Lord, all who by reason of infirmity or distance are hindered from worship in thy holy house. Let thy nearness be their recompense, and lead thy Church to seek out and visit the lonely, inasmuch as they are thine. (130)

THOSE IN PAIN

O God, who has exhalted the Crucified, thy Son, by a triumphant resurrection and ascension into heaven: may his triumphs and glories so shine in the eyes of our hearts and minds, that we may more clearly comprehend his sufferings, and more courageously pass through our own; for his sake who with thee and the Holy Ghost liveth and reigneth, one God, for ever and ever. (131)

We ask thee not, O Lord, to rid us of pain; but grant in thy mercy that our pain may be free from waste, unfretted by rebellion against thy will, unsoiled by thought of ourselves, purified by love of our kind and ennobled by devotion to thy kingdom, through the mercies of thine only Son, our Lord. (132)

O Lord, who dost feel the pain of the world, look down upon all sick and suffering persons; enfold them with thy love, that in the midst of pain they may find thy presence; to doctors and nurses grant tender hearts and healing hands; and give health again in body and soul, for thy tender mercy's sake. (133)

Grant, O Lord, to all those who are bearing pain, thy spirit of healing, thy spirit of peace and hope, of courage and endurance.

Cast out from them the spirit of anxiety and fear; grant them perfect confidence and trust in thee, that in thy light they may see light; through Jesus Christ our Lord. (134)

Good Jesu, physician of souls and bodies, make all sickness a healing medicine to the soul, soothe by thy presence each ache and pain; hallow all suffering by thine all-holy sufferings, and teach sufferers to unite their sufferings with thine, to be hallowed by thine; who livest. . . (135)

Ejaculatory Prayers for Those in Pain

Lord help them!

Support and strengthen them Lord!

Lord, help them to keep going!

My Lord and my God.

Lord, we offer all their pain against the terrible pain of the world.

Lord, we offer what they suffer for those who suffer without hope.

If you wish it, Lord, you can save them from suffering or you can cure them. We do not understand why you don't do something but if this is your will, so be it.

You bore the pain of the cross; please help them to bear this agony. (136)

READINGS WITH THOSE IN PAIN

Jesus then came with his disciples to a place called Gethsemane. He said to them, 'Sit here while I go over there to pray.'. . . He went on a little, fell on his face in prayer, and said, 'My Father, if it is possible, let this cup pass me by. Yet not as I will, but as thou wilt.'

. . . He went away a second time and prayed: 'My Father, if it is not possible for this cup to pass me by without my drinking it, thy will be done.' . . . So he left them and went away again; and he prayed the third time, using the same words as before.

(Matt. 26.36, 39, 42, 44)

For I reckon that the sufferings we now endure bear no comparison with the splendour, as yet unrevealed, which is in store for us. For the created universe waits with eager expectation for God's sons to be revealed. . . .because the universe itself is to be freed from the shackles of mortality and enter upon the liberty and splendour of the children of God. . . .we wait for God to make us his sons and set our whole body free. For we have been saved though only in hope. . . .if we hope for something we do not yet see, then, in waiting for it, we show our endurance.

(Rom. 8.18–19, 21, 23–24, 25)

. . . in me you may find peace. In the world you will have trouble. But courage! The victory is mine; I have conquered the world.

(John 16.33)

Since therefore we have a great high priest who has passed through the heavens, Jesus the Son of God, let us hold fast to the religion we profess. For ours is not a high priest unable to sympathize with our weaknesses, but one who, because of his likeness to us, has been tested every way, only without sin. Let us therefore boldly approach the throne of our gracious God, where we may receive mercy and in his grace find timely help.

(Heb. 4.14–16)

See also readings on pp. 62–3.

Suitable Psalms

Ps. 23 *The Lord is my shepherd*

Ps. 69. 1–3, 13–18, 30–37 *Save me, O God*

Ps. 77 *I will cry unto God with my voice*

Ps. 88 *O Lord God of my salvation*

Ps. 91 *Whoso dwelleth under the defence of the most High*

O God of mercy and of love, who by the blessed child-bearing of the Virgin Mary hast consecrated human motherhood, grant that she to whom thou hast given the promise of a child may dedicate herself day by day to the patient following of Jesus in the ways of holiness and peace, and by the grace of the Holy Spirit may be made worthy of the sacred trust which thy love has committed to her care; through Jesus Christ our Lord. (137)

After Childbirth

Thank you Lord for the safe arrival of our child, and for the care of doctors and nurses. We thank you for the gift of life and we ask that this child may enjoy a happy time in youth and a useful life of service; through Jesus Christ our Lord, who himself grew in wisdom and stature as well as in favour with God and men. (138)

Dear Jesus, help N. to realize the great gift which has been entrusted to her. Teach her to love and care for her baby, both in soul and body, as your mother treasured and guarded you – the incarnate Son of God. (139)

When a Baby has Died

O God, our heavenly Father, whose ways are hidden and works wonderful, comfort, we pray thee, this woman and her husband whose hearts are heavy with sorrow; surround them with thy protection, and grant them grace to face the future with good courage and hope. Teach them to use this pain in deeper sympathy for all who suffer, so that they may share in thy work of turning sorrow into joy; through Jesus Christ our Lord. (140)

PAEDIATRIC PATIENTS

O Heavenly Father, watch with us, we pray thee, over the sick child for whom our prayers are offered, and grant that *he* may be restored to that perfect health which it is thine alone to give; through Jesus Christ our Lord. (141)

O Lord Jesus Christ, Good Shepherd of the sheep, who dost gather the lambs with thine arms and carry them in thy bosom, we commit into thy loving hands this child. Relieve *his* pain, guard *him* from all danger, restore unto *him* the gifts of gladness and strength, and raise *him* up to a life of service to thee. Hear us, we beseech thee, for thy dear name's sake. (142)

O Lord Jesus Christ, who didst show on this earth thy love for children, and didst take them in thine arms, bless the children in this hospital; give to each one of them thy help in spirit and in body according to their needs; and grant that the lessons learned through patience and friendship here may bear fruit to their strengthening, to the enrichment of others, and to thine eternal glory. (143)

Heavenly Father, who didst send thy beloved Son into the world in the form of a little child, and to whom all children are dear, watch, we pray thee, with us over N. In thy mercy ease *his* suffering and restore *him* to health again. Bless those who minister to *his* needs, and give to us who wait the help of thy grace. (144)

See also *Prayers for Children*, Church Assembly Children's Council (C.I.O. 1968); *God is looking after me*, Church Assembly Children's Council (C.I.O. 1969).

READINGS WITH SICK CHILDREN

At that time the disciples came to Jesus and asked, 'Who is the greatest in the kingdom of Heaven?' He called a child, set him in front of them, and said, 'I tell you this: unless you turn round and become like children, you will never enter the kingdom of Heaven. Let a man humble himself till he is like this child, and he will be the greatest in the kingdom of Heaven.' (Matt. 18. 1–5)

They brought children for him to lay his hands on them with prayer. The disciples scolded them for it, but Jesus said to them, 'Let the children come to me: do not try to stop them, for the kingdom of Heaven belongs to such as these.' And he laid his hands on the children, and went his way. (Mat. 19. 13–15)

The chief priests and doctors of the law saw the wonderful things he did, and heard the boys in the temple shouting 'Hosanna to the Son of David!', and they asked him indignantly, 'Do you hear what they are saying?' Jesus answered, 'I do; have you never read that text, "Thou hast made children and babes at the breast sound aloud thy praise"?'. (Matt. 21. 15–16)

Then a man appeared – Jairus was his name and he was president of the synagogue. Throwing himself down at Jesus's feet he begged him to come to his house, because he had an only daughter, about twelve years old, who was dying. And while Jesus was on his way he could hardly breathe for the crowds . . . A man came from the president's house with the message, 'Your daughter is dead; trouble the Rabbi no further'. But Jesus heard, and interposed. 'Do not be afraid', he said; 'only show faith and she will be well again' . . . Jesus took hold of her hand and called her: 'Get up, my child.' Her spirit returned, she stood up immediately, and he told them to give her something to eat. Her parents were astounded; but he forbade them to tell anyone what had happened. (Luke 8.41–2; 49–50; 54–6)

Other suitable reading material is listed on p. 110.

THOSE ABOUT TO BE DISCHARGED

O God, who art everywhere present, look down in love upon all patients from here who are about to be discharged to their homes. Grant that, having learnt to know thee here, they may carry thine indwelling presence to their families and friends, and spread abroad thy light and thy love, and the happiness that comes from companionship with thee; through Jesus Christ our Lord. (145)

THOSE WHO HAVE BEEN DISCHARGED

O God,
Help those who have been discharged
 to avoid two things.
Help them to avoid
 trying to do too much
  in order to show how well they are,
 and so undoing all the good
  that has been done to them in hospital.
And help them to avoid
 acting as invalids,
  and expecting to be waited on hand and foot.
Give them a grateful heart
and a sensible mind,
 and help them to make steady progress,
  until they are fit again. (146)

CASUALTY PATIENTS

Jesus our brother, you also at the end despaired of the Father: raise up all who have fallen casualties through sickness, anxiety, bitterness, or fear, just as you did in your lifetime on earth; and unite them with us in one movement. (147)

O God, whose never-failing providence ordereth all things both in heaven and earth, mercifully look upon thy servant; succour and defend *him* from all evil; spare *him* that *he* may recover *his* strength; heal *him* of the injuries *he* has suffered; and allay the anxieties of *his* family; through Jesus Christ our Lord. (148)

ALCOHOLICS AND DRUG ADDICTS

O Lord Jesus Christ, who came not to condemn the world but to save men: look in mercy upon all drug addicts. Forgive the actions which have brought them into captivity. Release them from the thought of their next dose. Give them the will to accept a cure where such is possible, and restore to them the possibility of a healthy life; through Jesus Christ our Lord. (149)

Almighty Father, whose blessed Son refused at Calvary the deadening wine, have pity on all who use drugs to escape from their sorrows; by the virtue of his Cross give them grace to share his passion and his victory. (150)

Gracious Lord, the helper of all who put their trust in thee, we pray for those who are addicted to either alcohol or drugs, especially N. Give them, O Lord, the desire and the will to be free, and the grace to continue in the right way; and show us how to help them and lead them to thee, who art our hope and strength. (151)

THE SEXUALLY ILL

Most holy Lord, whose Word became incarnate and raised our fallen life from its degradation, have mercy upon all whose vital powers are beyond their present control and so unite them to yourself in chastity and love that their health may be restored; through him who triumphed in our flesh, the same Jesus Christ, who with you and the Holy Spirit shares the pure glory of eternal Godhead. (152)

THE MENTALLY ILL

Lord, we pray for the mentally ill,
  for all who are of a disturbed and troubled mind.
Be to them light in their darkness,
  their refuge and strength in time of fear.
Give special skills and tender hearts
  to all who care for them,
and show them how best to assist your work of healing,
  through Jesus Christ our Lord. (153)

Lord Jesus Christ, who for love of our souls entered the deep darkness of the cross:

we pray that your love may surround all who are in the darkness of great mental distress and who find it difficult to pray for themselves.

May they know that darkness and light are both alike to you and that you have promised never to fail them or forsake them. (154)

O Lord Jesus Christ, in your love and mercy, come and abide in the hearts of those who are burdened with anxiety and uncertainty, and whose minds are darkened; bring to them your mighty healing and light, that a new life may be opened to them in confidence and joy; for your name's sake. (155)

O Heavenly Father, who of thy love and wisdom knowest the anxieties and fears of thy children; whose Son Jesus Christ said to his disciples: 'It is I, be not afraid'; and to the tempest: 'Peace, be still'; grant that this thy servant may be strengthened to cast all *his* care upon thee, for thou carest for *him*. Give *him* quietness; give *him* unshaken trust; and may the day-spring from on high guide *his* feet into the way of peace; through the same Jesus Christ our Lord. (156)

O thou who art the Mind of all creation, we remember to our comfort that thou hast in thy special care all broken, outworn and imperfect minds. Give to those who live with them the understanding and loving Spirit of Christ. Enlighten those who are tempted to laugh at such infirmity, or regard it with shame. To all who are separated in this life by barriers of mental infirmity, grant the comfort of thy Holy Spirit, who with thee and thy Christ ever liveth and reigneth, one God, world without end. (157)

Lord of great compassion, we pray you for those who are nervously ill, and too weak and anxious to lift themselves above the fear and sadness that threaten to overwhelm them. Do you yourself, O Lord, lift them up and deliver them, as you delivered your disciples in the storm at sea, strengthening their faith and banishing their fear. Turning to you, O Lord, may they find you, and finding you may they find also all you have laid up for them within the fortress of your love. (158)

THE MENTALLY HANDICAPPED

O holy Spirit who dost search out all things, even the deep things of God and the deep things of man, we pray thee to penetrate into the springs of personality of all who are sick in mind, to bring them cleansing, healing, and unity. Sanctify all memory, dispel all fear, and bring them to love thee with all their mind and will, that they may be made whole and glorify thee for ever. We ask this in the name of him who cast out devils and healed men's minds, even Jesus Christ our Lord. (159)

THE MENTALLY INADEQUATE

O God of light and peace, give light and peace to all who are mentally inadequate. Give them courage and patience, and to those who help them, either in home or in hospital, skill, wisdom, and sympathy. Grant that they may always be cared for in love with a full understanding of their difficulties and limitations, that none may add to their troubles. We ask this in the name of him who succoured the distressed and troubled in mind, thy Son, Christ our Lord. (160)

THE PHYSICALLY HANDICAPPED

O loving Father, we pray for all who are handicapped in the race of life; the blind, the defective and the delicate, and all who are permanently injured. May they learn the mystery of the road of suffering which Christ has trodden and the saints have followed; and this we ask in the name of him who himself took our infirmities upon him, even the same Jesus Christ, our Saviour. (161)

THE ELDERLY SICK

Dear God, you made the whole of life to be lived and enjoyed, so please bless all old people. Give them all that they need for friendship, comfort and occupation. Above all give them zest for life and peace in their hearts; through Jesus Christ our Lord. (162)

O Lord God, who hast promised that they who wait upon thee shall renew their strength, and that as their days so shall their strength be: comfort thou them according unto thy word; cast them not away in the time of age, and forsake them not when their strength faileth; make thy face to shine upon thy servant, and at evening time it shall be light, through Jesus Christ our Lord. (163)

Jesus, who never grew old, it is not easy for any of us to face old age. It is fine to be young, attractive, strong. Old age reminds us of weakness and dependence upon others. But to be your disciple means accepting weakness and interdependence. Because of you we can rejoice in weakness in ourselves, and be tender to it in others. (164)

O Lord Jesus Christ, who didst hear the prayer of thy two disciples and abide with them, when it was toward evening and the day was far spent, abide, we pray thee, with thine aged servants in the evening of life. Make thyself known unto them as their companion and friend, and bring them safe to their eternal home. (165)

THOSE WHO NURSE THEM

Give them, O Lord, thy spirit of patience and perseverance in all their dealings with the frail and fragile; and at times when faith is difficult and work is hard grant them the help of thy grace to keep them from falling and to present them at last without fault before thy throne. (166)

THOSE WHO ARE LOSING HOPE

Comfort we beseech thee, most gracious God, all who are cast down and faint of heart amidst the sorrows and difficulties of the world; grant that by the energy of thy Holy Spirit they may be enabled to go upon their way rejoicing and give thee continual thanks for thy sustaining providence; through Jesus Christ, our Saviour. (167)

Lord, when it is dark and we cannot feel your presence, and nothing seems real any more, and we are tempted to give up trying, help us to remember that you are never really absent and to trust you still; so may we rest in your love, and know that underneath are the everlasting arms. (168)

O Lord, who shouldered the strain and the stress of life, be with those who because of their burdens go down into the pit of disturbance and depression. When things are black and hopeless stretch out your hand to hold them firm. Give them courage to climb upwards to the light of this world's day, and of your love; through Jesus Christ our Lord. (169)

Shine in the hearts and minds of those who think themselves forgotten by thee, O God. Hear our prayers for all who are in spiritual darkness and the shadow of what is worse than death, and in thy mercy guide their steps into the ways of thy peace. (170)

Defend with thy strength, O God, all those who, overcome by the difficulties and perplexities of life, are losing hope. Give them a new vision of thy love, that they may see again what they fear to have lost, and grant that what they see they may long for, trusting in thee for its fulfilment. (171)

O Almighty God, reveal the power of thy grace to all who are in despair; that those who have ceased to hope may begin to trust, and those who have lost all other confidence may be brought, even by despair, to confide in thee, who canst make all things new. (172)

READINGS WITH THOSE LOSING HOPE

Come to me, all whose work is hard. . . (see p.19).

Set your troubled hearts at rest. Trust in God always; trust also in me. There are many dwelling-places in my Father's house; if it were not so I should have told you; for I am going there on purpose to prepare a place for you. And if I go and prepare a place for you, I shall come again and receive you to myself, so that where I am you may be also. (John 14.1–4)

‘I came from the Father and have come into the world. Now I am leaving the world again and going to the Father.’ His disciples said, ‘Why, this is plain speaking; this is no figure of speech. We are certain now that you know everything, and do not need to be questioned; because of this we believe that you have come from God.’ Jesus answered, ‘Do you now believe? Look, the hour is coming, has indeed already come, when you are all to be scattered, each to his home, leaving me alone. Yet I am not alone, because the Father is with me.’ (John 16.28–32)

Praise be to the God and Father of our Lord Jesus Christ, the all-merciful Father, the God whose consolation never fails us! He comforts us in all our troubles, so that we in turn may be able to comfort others in any trouble of theirs and to share with them the consolation we ourselves receive from God. (2 Cor. 1.3–4)

And the God of all grace, who called you into his eternal glory in Christ, will himself, after your brief suffering, restore, establish, and strengthen you on a firm foundation. He holds dominion for ever and ever. Amen. (1 Pet. 5.10–11)

Let us continue at peace with God through our Lord Jesus Christ, through whom we have been allowed to enter the sphere of God’s grace, where we now stand. Let us exult in the hope of the divine splendour that is to be ours. More than this: let us even exult in our present sufferings, because we know that suffering trains us to endure, and endurance brings proof that we have stood the test, and this proof is the ground of hope. Such a hope is no mockery, because God’s love has flooded our inmost heart through the Holy Spirit he has given us. (Rom. 5.1–5)

Suitable Psalms

Ps. 22 *My God, my God. . . why hast thou forsaken me. . .?*
Ps. 38 *Put me not to rebuke*
Ps. 42.1, 5–8, 11 *Like as the hart desireth. . .*
Ps. 86 *Bow down thine ear, O Lord*

THE DEAF

O God, our heavenly Father, whose dearly beloved Son Jesus Christ went about doing good, unstopping the ears of the deaf and loosening the tongues of the dumb; look down with loving eyes upon all thy deaf and mute children, and give them the special blessing of thy mercy and grace; that they may learn the truth as it is in Jesus and find in him their joy and peace. Grant this, O Father, for Jesus Christ's sake. (173)

Almighty God, in whose Holy Word there is promise of a day when the eyes of the blind shall be opened, the ears of the deaf shall be unstopped, and the tongue of the dumb shall sing; of thy mercy, we beseech thee for all who now live in darkness or in silence. Fortify them to bear their affliction with unwavering faith; grant to them that inner sight and hearing ear to which thy truth and beauty are ever revealed; and may they know thee as their constant friend and guide. (174)

O Lord, we pray thee, look with compassion on those who are deaf, and grant that they who by reason of their affliction are deprived of so much of the interest of life may in their difficulties know thee always present with them; and of thy mercy, Lord, help us that we may not fail them in sympathy and patience; through Jesus Christ our Lord. (175)

THE BLIND

Lord Christ, when you gave sight to the blind in your ministry on earth you spoke about a greater power of inward sight: we pray that those who cannot see the world about them may perceive the things of eternal worth, and receive from those near to them a friendship and care which will help them to overcome their handicap and will be a light to their path. (176)

O God, who hast sent thy Son to be the true light, grant that they who cannot see the things of this world may be the more enlightened and comforted by his inward guidance. Cheer them in their blindness with the sense of thy presence, that, beholding thee with increasing love, they may be conformed to thy likeness, until they see thee as thou art, and awake to the full revelation of thy glory; through the same Jesus Christ our Lord. (177)

O God, who art the Father of light, with whom is no darkness at all: we thank thee for the good gift of sight which thou hast bestowed upon us. Fill us, we pray thee, with thine own compassion for those who have it not; direct and prosper the efforts that are made for their welfare: reveal to them by thy Spirit the things which eye hath not seen, and comfort them with the hope of light everlasting; to which, of thy great mercy, we beseech thee to bring us all; through Jesus Christ our Saviour. (178)

O God, whose voice at creation called light to shine out of the darkness: We praise you for the gift of sight and for the wealth of beauty shared by those who see. Give us the compassion of your Son, our Saviour, who by his love and mercy gave sight to the blind. Let your healing touch bless all the ministries for restoring sight. May your light shine within our hearts, leading us by the power of your Spirit. (179)

O God, the source of all light, lighten the darkness of those who have no sight, illuminate their inward vision, and let them rest in thee, for the sake of Jesus Christ our Lord. (180)

THE SLEEPLESS AND RESTLESS

Gracious and most merciful Father; let Thy presence and peace be known wheresoever there is sickness, sorrow or distress. Give to all tired and weary sufferers, this night, the gift of sleep; and, if sleep come not, let Thy Holy Spirit bring to their remembrance thoughts of comfort from Thy Word, that they may stay their minds on Thee, through Jesus Christ our Lord. (181)

Close the eyes of the wakeful, most blessed Lord, with thy gentle touch, giving them the rest and security that abide in thy nearness, O thou in whom there is no night and no darkness.(182)

O Holy spirit, bless all who have sleepless nights, and grant them patience, and fill their hearts with peace, for Jesus' sake. (183)

Save us while waking, and defend us while sleeping, that when we awake we may watch with Christ, and when we sleep we may rest in peace. (184)

Lord Jesus, who in thy passion was spent with pain and weariness, hear us and grant, if it be thy will, the rest of quiet sleep to this thy servant. Grant that in the quiet watches of the night *his* soul may be so stayed on thee that *he* may continually praise and bless thy holy name. (185)

THOSE WHO HAVE NO-ONE TO PRAY FOR THEM

O God of love, who art in all places and times, pour thy spirit of healing and comfort upon every lonely heart. Have pity upon those who are bereft of human love, and on those to whom it has never come. Be unto them a strong consolation, and in the end give them the fullness of joy; for the sake of Jesus Christ our Lord. (186)

Accept our prayers, O Lord, for all those who have no one to love them enough to pray for them. Wherever and whoever they are, give them a share of thy blessings, and in thy love let them know that they are not forgotten. (187)

Visit with thy presence, O Lord, those who live alone, and grant them friendly neighbours, help in time of need, and the joy of fellowship in thy Church. (188)

READINGS WITH THE LONELY AND FRIENDLESS

You are my friends, if you do what I command you. I call you servants no longer; a servant does not know what his master is about. I have called you friends, because I have disclosed to you everything that I heard from my Father. You did not chose me: I chose you. I appointed you to go on and bear fruit, fruit that shall last; so that the Father may give you all that you ask in my name. (John 15.14–16)

In everything, as we know, he co-operates for good with those who love God and are called according to his purpose. . . With all this in mind, what are we to say? If God is on our side, who is against us? He did not spare his own Son, but gave him up for us all; and with this gift how can he fail to lavish upon us all he has to give? (Rom. 8.28, 31, 32)

God be praised, he gives us the victory through our Lord Jesus Christ. Therefore, my beloved brothers, stand firm and immovable, and work for the Lord always, work without limit, since you know that in the Lord your labour cannot be lost. (1 Cor. 15.57–58)

How great is the love that the Father has shown to us! We were called God's children, and such we are; and the reason why the godless world does not recognize us is that it has not known him. Here and now, dear friends, we are God's children; what we shall be has not yet been disclosed, but we know that when it is disclosed we shall be like him, because we shall see him as he is. Everyone who has this hope before him purifies himself, as Christ is pure. (1 John 3.1–3)

John 16.32, 33 (See pp. 72, 83).

Suitable Psalms

Ps. 13 *How long wilt thou forget me, O Lord*
Ps. 20 *The Lord hear thee in the day of trouble*

Ps. 23 *The Lord is my shepherd*
Ps. 71.2, 4, 8, 11, 17 *In thee, O Lord, have I put my trust*
Ps. 86 *Bow down thine ear, O Lord, and hear me*
Ps. 130 *Out of the deep have I called unto thee*
Ps. 142 *I cried unto the Lord with my voice*

THE UNCONSCIOUS

O heavenly Father, who in thy love and wisdom knowest the anxieties and fears of thy children, grant that this thy servant may be enabled to cast all *his* cares upon thee, for thou carest for *him*. Give *him* quietness of mind and unshaken trust in thee, and guide *his* feet into the way of peace; through Jesus Christ our Lord. (189)

CANCER PATIENTS

O God, mighty giver of life, you are able to sustain what you have created: we ask you to heal the ills of those who suffer from the threat of cancer. We ask you to restore the physical body and also to cleanse the mind of the ills of worry, fear and despair, that both health of body and joy of soul may unite to undergird and uplift those who suffer, and so place them within the range of your healing power; through Jesus Christ, our Lord. (190)

THE SEEMINGLY INCURABLE

Heavenly Father, we pray for those who suffer from incurable diseases.

May they remember always that their infirmities are of the physical body which withers away, and come to discover that their condition can be a way through difficulty to a deeper awareness of the life of the spirit.

Through the pain and weariness of illness may they know that they are not alone, and in fellowship with Christ learn to understand better the sufferings of others. (191)

Heavenly Father, to whom the needs of every heart are known, let the cry of your children come to you; and look in mercy on all who are beyond human help, all whose hope is gone, all whose sickness finds no cure. Give them your strength, O God, to endure with courage and patience, and let your presence dispel all fear, through Jesus Christ our Lord. (192)

Almighty God, whose grace is sufficient
  for all our need,
and whose power comes to full strength
  in our weakness:
we pray for all who suffer
  and who never get well,
that sustained in their weakness
  and released from pain,
they may rejoice in the power of Christ
  resting upon them.
We ask this in his name. (193)

O Lord, who dost feel the pain of the world; look with mercy, we beseech thee, upon those who in their sickness and suffering are beyond the reach of human skill. To thee alone belongs the power of life, and these souls are thine. If in the mystery of thy providence it shall be their lot to bear their infirmity to the end, then, Lord, of thy love give them grace to endure bravely, and such an assurance of thy presence with them in it that they may, like their Saviour, be made perfect through suffering. (194)

O heavenly Father, we pray for those suffering from diseases for which at present there is no cure. Give them the victory of trust and hope, that they may never lose their faith in thy loving purpose. Grant thy wisdom to all who are working to discover the causes of disease, and the realization that through thee all things are possible. We ask this in the name of him who went about doing good and healing all manner of disease; even thy Son, Jesus Christ our Lord. (195)

THE DYING

O Lord Jesus Christ, who in thy last agony didst commend thy spirit into the hands of thy heavenly Father: have mercy upon all sick and dying persons; may death be unto them the gate of everlasting life; and give them the assurance of thy presence even in the dark valley; for thy name's sake who art the resurrection and the life, and to whom be glory for ever and ever. (196)

O Saviour Divine, into thy loving and merciful hands we commend the souls of the dying. By thy most precious death which was our life, forsake not thy servants who have now none other helper beside thee. Receive their spirits, and bring them into thy presence, that the darkness may light about them, and that they may behold thy face in righteousness and be satisfied when they wake with thy likeness. Hear our cry we humbly beseech thee, O Lord Christ. (197)

EJACULATORY PRAYERS WITH THE DYING

Forsake me not, when my strength faileth me.

Into thy hands I commend my spirit; for thou hast redeemed me, O Lord, thou God of truth.

Yea, though I walk through the valley of the shadow of death, I will fear no evil; for thou art with me; thy rod and thy staff comfort me.

With thee is the well of life; and in thy light shall we see light.

Thou shalt show me the path of life; in thy presence is the fullness of joy; and at thy right hand there is pleasure for evermore.

As for me, I will behold thy presence in righteousness; and when I awake up after thy likeness, I shall be satisfied with it.

(*from the Psalms*)

God so loved the world that he gave his only begotten Son, that whosoever believeth in him should not perish, but have everlasting life.

I am the Good Shepherd; the good shepherd giveth his life for the sheep.

Let not your heart be troubled: ye believe in God; believe also in me. In my Father's house are many mansions.

Because I live, ye shall live also. (*from St John's Gospel*)

Whether we live, we live unto the Lord: or whether we die, we die unto the Lord: whether we live, therefore, or die, we are the Lord's.

Eye hath not seen, nor ear heard, neither have entered into the heart of man, the things which God hath prepared for them that love him.

Now we see through a glass darkly; but then face to face; now I know in part; but then I shall know even as also I am known.

O death, where is thy sting? O grave, where is thy victory?

Thanks be to God which giveth us the victory through our Lord Jesus Christ.

We look not at the things which are seen, but at the things which are not seen; for the things which are seen are temporal, but the things which are not seen are eternal. (*from the Epistles*)

NOTE
The New Testament readings above are from the more familiar versions.

COMMENDATION OF THE DYING

Unto thee, O Lord, we commend the soul of this thy servant, that, dying to the world, *he* may live to thee; and whatsoever sins *he* has committed through the frailty of earthly life, do thou clear away by thy most loving and merciful forgiveness, through Jesus Christ our Lord.

Depart, O Christian soul, out of the world,
In the name of God, the Almighty Father, who created thee;
In the name of Jesus Christ, his Son, who redeemed thee;
In the name of the Holy Ghost, who sanctifieth thee.
May thy guardian angel succour and defend thee;
May the prayers of the blessed saints help thee;
May thy Redeemer look upon thee in pardon and mercy;
May thy portion be peace, and thy rest with him this day in Paradise.

Short Commendations

Lord, now lettest thou thy servant depart in peace.

This day shalt thou be with me in paradise.

Into thy hands we commend *his* spirit, for thou hast redeemed *him*, thou God of truth.

Embrace *him* with the arms of thy mercy, and give *him* an inheritance with thy saints in light and joy, in glory and happiness, for ever and ever.

THE DEPARTED

O Lord our God, from Whom neither life nor death can separate those who trust in Thy love, and whose love holds in its embrace Thy children in this world and in the next: so unite us to Thyself that in fellowship with Thee we may be always united to our loved ones whether here or there; give us courage, constancy, and hope; through Him who died and was buried and rose again for us, Jesus Christ our Lord. (198)

O Eternal Lord God, who holdest all souls in life; we beseech thee to shed forth upon thy whole Church in paradise and on earth the bright beams of thy light and heavenly comfort; that we, following the good example of those who have loved and served thee here and are now at rest, may with them at length enter into the fullness of thine unending joy; through Jesus Christ our Lord. (199)

Into thy hands, O God, we commend the souls of all our loved ones (especially . . .) as into the hands of a faithful Creator and most loving Saviour; beseeching thee to grant unto them pardon and peace and, of thine infinite goodness, wisdom and power, to work in them the good purpose of thy perfect will; through Jesus Christ our Lord. (200)

Quicken, O Lord, our departed in thy compassion, and set them at thy right hand. Clothe them with excellent glory in thy kingdom, and join them to the just and righteous who fulfil thy will in Jerusalem which is above: O Lord of our death and our life, Father, Son and Holy Spirit for ever. (201)

O Almighty God, the God of the spirits of all flesh, multiply, we beseech thee, to those who sleep in Jesus, the manifold blessings of thy love, that the good work which thou didst begin in them may be perfected unto the day of Jesus Christ. And of thy mercy, O heavenly Father, vouchsafe that we, who now serve thee here on earth, may at the last, together with them, be found meet to be partakers of the inheritance of the saints in light; for the sake of the same thy Son, Jesus Christ our Lord and Saviour. (202)

BEFORE VISITING THOSE WHO MOURN

Lord, teach me what to say when I go to visit those who have just been bereaved. I feel utterly powerless in the face of their grief. They have to suffer so much. I am distressed for them, but words seem to fail me. Act through me, and make me the instrument of your comfort even if I say very little. Give me understanding compassion and give them faith in your strength, and peace so as to be able to endure their pain and loneliness which is so very deep. O Help of the helpless, help us all in our distress for the sake of your Son who knew the depths of human suffering. (203)

THOSE WHO MOURN

O God, our only help in time of need, be close to me in my sorrow, in your mercy give me strength to keep going, and help me to trust you whatever happens and increase my love. Into your loving hands I commend myself and the soul of . . . ; give us peace and rest in you. (204)

Almighty God, whose Son our Lord Jesus Christ won the victory over death: grant that all who mourn the loss of those dear to them may enter into his victory, and find comfort, hope and peace in him, who is the resurrection and the life. (205)

O thou in whose house are many mansions, speak through me to those whose loved one has gone from their sight, but not from thine. There is nothing in me to heal the wounded heart or fill the aching void. But let thy words of comfort and truth be given to me to speak that these sorrowing ones may find their peace in thee; through Jesus Christ our Lord. (206)

O Heavenly Father, whose blessed Son Jesus Christ did weep at the grave of Lazarus, look, we beseech thee, with compassion upon those who are now in sorrow and affliction; comfort them, O Lord, with thy gracious consolations; make them to know that all things work together for good to them that love thee; and grant them evermore sure trust and confidence in thy fatherly care; through Jesus Christ our Lord. (207)

Grant, O Lord, to all who are bereaved the spirit of faith and courage, that they may have strength to meet the days to come with steadfastness and patience; not sorrowing as those without hope, but in thankful remembrance of thy great goodness in past years, and in the sure expectation of a joyful reunion with those they love; and this we ask in the name of Jesus Christ our Saviour. (208)

O God, please be very close to all those who are mourning for the loss of someone they loved. May you be their comfort and their strength; through Jesus Christ our Lord. (209)

READINGS WITH THOSE WHO MOURN

The souls of the righteous are in the hand of God, And no torment shall touch them . . . they are in peace. (Wisd. 3.1,3)

Jesus said, 'I am the resurrection and I am life. If a man has faith in me, even though he die, he shall come to life; and no one who is alive and has faith shall ever die. Do you believe this?' 'Lord, I do,' she answered; 'I now believe that you are the Messiah, the Son of God who was to come into the world.' (John 11.25–7)

John 14.1–4 (See p. 82).
Rom. 8.35, 37–9 (See p. 65).
1. Cor. 15.55–8 (See p. 87).

All that the Father gives me will come to me, and the man who comes to me I will never turn away. I have come down from heaven, not to do my own will, but the will of him who sent me. It is his will that I should not lose even one of all that he has given me, but raise them all up on the last day. For it is my Father's will that everyone who looks upon the Son and puts his faith in him shall possess eternal life; and I will raise him up on the last day. (John 6.37–40)

This day, Master, thou givest thy servant his discharge in peace; now thy promise is fulfilled. (Luke 2.29)

Suitable Psalms

Ps. 23 *The Lord is my shepherd*
Ps. 27.1–7 *The Lord is my light and my salvation*
Ps. 121 *I will lift up mine eyes unto the hills*
Ps. 123 *Unto thee lift I up mine eyes*
Ps. 130 *Out of the deep have I called unto thee*

THE COMMUNION OF SAINTS

Grant, O Lord, that in the communion of saints, we may become true companions of them that have loved thee in this life, and with them keep thy commandments unto the end; through Jesus Christ our Lord. (210)

Lord, help us to perceive that we are all linked together through you, and that because of our union with you, we share each others' burdens and joys. Lord, make us realise that we are never alone in suffering for you and all our brothers are with us in it. By our prayers for each other made through you and by the prayers of the saints on earth and in heaven, make us conscious of the great support we have as members of your Body. Lord, I thank you for the most wonderful gift of the communion of Saints. (211)

O God, who hast brought us near to an innumerable company of angels, and to the spirits of just men made perfect, grant us during our earthly pilgrimage to abide in thy fellowship, and in our heavenly country to become partakers of thy joy; through Jesus Christ our Lord. (212)

MEMORIALS

Bring us, O Lord God, at our last awakening into the house and gate of heaven, to enter into that gate and dwell in that house, where there shall be no darkness nor dazzling, but one equal light; no noise nor silence, but one equal music; no fears nor hopes, but one equal possession; no ends nor beginnings, but one equal eternity; in the habitations of thy majesty and thy glory, world without end. (213)

Stephen, filled with the Holy Spirit, gazed into heaven and saw the glory of God, and Jesus standing at God's right hand. 'I can see heaven thrown open', he said, 'and the Son of man standing at the right hand of God'. (214)

Remember, O Lord, thy servants who have departed hence in the Lord, especially N. and all others to whom our remembrance is due. Give them eternal rest and peace in thy heavenly kingdom, and to us such a measure of communion with them as thou knowest to be best for us; through Jesus Christ our Lord. (215)

Grant, O Lord, that keeping in glad remembrance those who have gone before, who have stood by us and helped us, who have cheered us by their sympathy and strengthened us by their example, we may seize every opportunity of life and rejoice in the promise of a glorious resurrection with them; through Jesus Christ our Lord. (216)

For thy servants departed this life in thy faith and fear; for the memory of their words and example; for the sure and certain hope of reunion with them hereafter; for the happiness that is theirs, and for our communion with them, we give thanks to thee, O God. (217)

AFFIRMATIONS

In the world you will have trouble. But courage! The victory is mine; I have conquered the world. (John 16.22)

For Love

This is my commandment: love one another as I have loved you. (John 15.12)

God loved the world so much that he gave his only Son, that everyone who has faith in him may not die but have eternal life. (John 3.16)

God is love; he who dwells in love is dwelling in God, and God in him. (1 John 4.16)

For Peace of Mind

. . . in everything, as we know, he co-operates for good with those who love God and are called according to his purpose. (Rom 8.28)

. . . be assured, I am with you always, to the end of time. (Matt.28.20)

Thou wilt keep him in perfect peace, whose mind is stayed on thee: because he trusteth in thee. (Isa.26.3)

In Desolation

Do not be afraid, only have faith. (Mark 5.36)

O give me the comfort of thy help again. (Ps. 61.12)

Out of the deep have I called unto thee, O Lord. (Ps. 130.1)

Come to me, all whose work is hard, whose load is heavy; and I will give you relief. (Matt. 11.28)

Trust in God

The Lord is the strength of my life; whom then shall I fear? (Ps. 27.1)

I will lift up mine eyes unto the hills, from whence cometh my help.
My help cometh even from the Lord, who hath made heaven and earth. (Ps. 121.1–2)

Set your troubled hearts at rest, and banish your fears. (John 14.27)

For Courage

Be strong, and of a good courage; be not afraid, neither be thou dismayed: for the Lord thy God is with thee whithersoever thou goest. (Josh. 1.9)

I have come that men may have life, and may have it in all its fullness. (John 10.10)

When Prayer is Difficult

Lord, teach me to pray. (Luke 11.1)

Lord, open thou my lips. (Ps. 51.15)

The spirit is willing, but the flesh is weak. (Mark 14.38)

Be still . . . and know that I am God. (Ps. 46.10)

For Faith

I have faith . . . help me where faith falls short. (Mark 9.24)

Lord, increase my faith. (Luke 17.5)

If God is on our side, who is against us? (Rom. 8.31)

Nevertheless, though I am sometime afraid, yet put I my trust in thee. (Ps. 56.3)

Sorrow for Sin

Make me a clean heart, O God: and renew a right spirit within me. (Ps. 51.10)

Son of David, Jesus, have pity on me. (Mark 10.47)

See also pp. 66–7.

EJACULATORY PRAYERS

In Sickness

I will come and heal him.

O Lord, heal me. Speak the word only and I shall be healed.

When Lying Sleepless

Peace, be still.

Our life is hid with Christ.

The Lord is nigh unto all them that call upon him.

Take me under the covering of thy wings, and let thy loving-kindness and thy truth always preserve me.

Preserve my lying down and my rising up, from this time forth and for evermore.

When Lying Awake in Pain

Hold thou my hands.

Help me to bear my pain, and to suffer for thee.

O turn this pain into joy, and give me rest in thee.

O Lord, by thy cross and passion strengthen me.

Lord, let this cup pass from me; nevertheless, not my will but thine be done.

When in Spiritual Deadness

Why art thou so full of heaviness, O my soul, and why art thou so disquieted within me? Put thy trust in God: for I will yet give him thanks for the help of his countenance.

O show me the light of thy countenance, and I shall be made whole.

In Difficulty and Danger

O Saviour of the world, who by thy cross and precious blood hast redeemed us; save us and help us, we humbly beseech thee, O Lord.

Our help is in the name of the Lord.

For Guidance

Thy will be done.

With thee is the well of life; and in thy light we shall see light.

Short Thanksgivings

Glory be to thee, O Lord, for thy mercy.

What reward shall I give unto the Lord: for all the benefits that he hath done unto me?

I will thank thee, for thou hast heard me: and art become my salvation.

For Use at any Time

O Good Jesu, my God and my all, keep me ever near thee. Let nothing for a moment separate me from thee.

Good Jesu, strength of the weary, rest of the restless; by the weariness and unrest of thy sacred cross, come to me who am weary that I may rest in thee.

Jesus most tender, in thee would I trust; let me never be confounded.

Good Jesu, who hast borne so patiently with me, make me wholly patient for love of thee.

See also p. 71.

THANKSGIVING PRAYERS

O Lord, by whom all souls live; we thank Thee for those whom Thy love has called from the life of trial to the life of rest. We trust them to Thy care; we pray Thee that by Thy grace we may be brought to enjoy with them the endless life of glory; through Jesus Christ our Lord. (218)

O God, we wish to thank you for the many mercies granted to us during our stay in hospital; for our restoration to health, friendships made, and opportunities given to learn our dependence upon you and all who have ministered to our needs. (219)

Most gracious God and Father, we render thee humble thanks for the restoration to health of thy servant N., for whom this congregation besought thy loving-kindness; and joyfully do we confess that as thy majesty is infinite, so also is thy mercy toward them that call upon thee for succour, in the name of thy son Jesus Christ our Lord. (220)

O God, whose love we cannot measure and whose blessings are without number, we bless and praise thee for all thy goodness, who in our weakness art our strength, in our darkness light, in our sorrows comfort and peace, and from everlasting to everlasting art our God, Father, Son, and Holy Spirit, world without end. (221)

EJACULATORY PRAYERS OF THANKSGIVING

I will give thanks unto the Lord with my whole heart, secretly among the faithful and in the congregation.

Praise the Lord, O my soul; and all that is within me praise his holy name.

Thou art my God, and I will praise thee.

Not unto us, O Lord, not unto us, but unto thy name be the praise.

O praise the Lord, for it is a good thing to sing praises unto our God; yea, a joyful and pleasant thing it is to be thankful.

READINGS OF THANKSGIVING

Phil. 4.6–7 (See p. 62).

. . . let the Holy Spirit fill you: speak to one another in psalms, hymns, and songs; sing and make music in your hearts to the Lord; and in the name of our Lord Jesus Christ give thanks every day for everything to our God and Father. (Eph. 5.18–20)

Let Christ's peace be arbiter in your hearts; to this peace you were called as members of a single body. And be filled with gratitude. Let the message of Christ dwell among you in all its richness. Instruct and admonish each other with the utmost wisdom. Sing thankfully in your hearts to God . . . Whatever you are doing, whether you speak or act, do everything in the name of the Lord Jesus, giving thanks to God the Father through him.

(Col. 3.15–17)

Suitable Psalms

Ps. 30 *I will magnify thee, O Lord*
Ps. 34 *I will alway give thanks unto the Lord*
Ps. 40 *I waited patiently for the Lord*
Ps. 63 *O God, thou art my God: early will I seek thee*
Ps. 100 *O be joyful in the Lord*
Ps. 103 *Praise the Lord, O my soul*
Ps. 111. 1–4 *I will give thanks unto the Lord*
Ps. 116 11–16 *I am well pleased*
Ps. 118 1–6 *O give thanks unto the Lord*
Ps. 138 *I will give thanks unto thee, O Lord*
Ps. 145 *I will magnify thee, O God, my King*
Ps. 150 *O praise God in his holiness*

BENEDICTIONS

The grace of our Lord Jesus Christ, and the love of God, and the fellowship of the Holy Spirit, be with us all evermore. (222)

Grace to you and peace from God the Father, and our Lord Jesus Christ. (223)

The God of hope fill you with all joy and peace in believing, so that by the power of the Holy Spirit you may abound in hope. (224)

The grace of our Lord Jesus Christ be with you all. (225)

May the God of peace, who brought again from the dead our Lord Jesus, the great shepherd of the sheep, equip you with everything good, that you may do his will, working in you that which is pleasing in his sight, through Jesus Christ, to whom be glory for ever and ever. (226)

The God of all grace, who has called you to his eternal glory in Christ, restore, establish, and strengthen you. To him be the dominion for ever and ever. (227)

Now to him who by the power at work within us is able to do far more abundantly than all that we ask or think, to him be glory in the Church and in Christ Jesus to all generations, for ever and ever. (228)

Now to him who is able to keep you from falling, and to present you without blemish before the presence of his glory with rejoicing, to the only God our Saviour, be glory and majesty, might and authority, through Jesus Christ our Lord, before all time, now, and for evermore. (229)

To the King of ages, immortal, invisible, the only God, be honour and glory for ever and ever. (230)

The God of peace himself sanctify you wholly; and may your spirit and soul and body be preserved entire, without blame at the coming of our Lord Jesus Christ. (231)

Blessing and glory and wisdom and thanksgiving and honour and power and might be to our God for ever and ever. (232)

The peace of God, which passes all understanding, keep your hearts and minds in the knowledge and love of God, and of his Son Jesus Christ our Lord; and the blessing of God almighty, the Father, the Son, and the Holy Spirit, be among you, and remain with you always. (233)

To God's gracious mercy and protection we commit you.
The Lord bless you and keep you.
The Lord make his face to shine upon you and be gracious to you.
The Lord lift up his countenance upon you, and give you peace.
(234)

May the blessing of God almighty, the Father, the Son, and the Holy Spirit, rest upon you; may he give light to guide you, courage to support you, and love to unite you, now and evermore. (235)

May the love of the Lord Jesus draw you to himself;
may the power of the Lord Jesus strengthen you in his service;
may the joy of the Lord Jesus fill your souls;
and the blessing of God almighty, the Father, the Son, and the Holy Spirit, be upon you and remain with you for ever. (236)

Go forth into the world in peace; be of good courage; hold fast that which is good; render to no man evil for evil; strengthen the faint-hearted; support the weak; help the afflicted; honour all men; love and serve the Lord, rejoicing in the power of the Holy Spirit. And the blessing of God almighty, the Father, the Son, and the Holy Spirit, be upon you, and remain with you for ever.
(237)

Blessing and honour and thanksgiving and praise,
more than we can utter,
more than we can conceive,
be yours, O holy and glorious Trinity,
Father, Son, and Holy Spirit,
by all angels, all men, all creatures,
for ever and ever. (238)

To God the Father, who loved us, and made us accepted in the Beloved;
to God the Son, who loved us, and washed us from our sins by his own blood;
to God the Holy Spirit, who sheds the love of God abroad in our hearts:
to the one true God be all love and all glory, for time and for eternity. (239)

The almighty and merciful Lord, the Father, the Son, and the Holy Spirit, bless and preserve us. (240)

May grace, mercy, and peace, from God the Father, Son, and Holy Spirit, be with you all, this day and for evermore. (241)

May the Lord bless you, and preserve you from all evil, and bring you to everlasting life. (242)

May the blessing of God almighty, the Father, the Son, and the Holy Spirit, rest upon you and upon your homes, this day and evermore. (243)

May the blessing of the Lord rest upon you and upon all his people, in every land, of every tongue, now and evermore. (244)

Now unto him who is able to do exceeding abundantly above all that we ask or think according to the power that worketh in us, unto him be glory in the Church and in Christ Jesus throughout all ages, world without end. (245)

May the God of all grace who hath called us unto his eternal glory by Christ Jesus, after that we have suffered awhile, make us perfect, stablish, strengthen us. To him be glory and dominion for ever and ever. (246)

Now unto God the Father, God the Son, and God the Holy Spirit be ascribed, as is most justly due, all honour, power, might, majesty, and dominion henceforth and for evermore. (247)

The Almighty God, the Father of our Lord Jesus Christ, of whom the whole family in heaven and earth is named, grant you to be strengthened with might by his Spirit in the inner man; that Christ dwelling in your hearts by faith, ye may be filled with all the fulness of God. (248)

May God bless us all with a loving sense of his near presence, to guide us, to protect us, and to help us; and may we know what it is to walk close with him all our life long. (249)

May God be within us to refresh us, around us to protect us, before us to guide us, above us to bless us, beneath us to hold us up; who liveth and reigneth, one God, world without end. (250)

Blessed be the Lord God, even the God of Israel: which only doeth wondrous things;
And blessed be the Name of his majesty for ever; and all the earth shall be filled with his majesty. (251)

The Lord preserve our going out, and our coming in: from this time forth for evermore. (252)

Blessed be the name of God for ever and ever. (253)

Blessed is God that liveth for ever; and blessed is his kingdom. (254)

Unto him that loved us, and washed us from our sins in his own blood, And hath made us kings and priests unto God and his Father, unto him be glory and dominion, for ever and ever. (255)

Blessing, and honour, and glory, and power be unto him that sitteth upon the throne, and unto the Lamb for ever and ever. (256)

A SELECTION OF READING MATERIAL

The priest will have his own list of readings which have a special appeal to him personally, and which he has found particularly helpful in his ministry. The following books are selections merely listed for reference and information:

A Year of Grace, ed. Victor Gollancz. Gollancz 1964.

From Darkness to Light, ed. Victor Gollancz. Gollancz 1956.

The Art of Prayer: An Orthodox Anthology, compiled by Iguman Chariton of Valamo. Faber 1966.

The Way of a Pilgrim, tr. R.M. French. S.P.C.K. 1965.

A Book of Comfort, Elizabeth Goudge. Fontana Books 1968.

A Book of Peace, Elizabeth Goudge. Hodder & Stoughton 1972.

A Diary of Prayer, Elizabeth Goudge, Hodder & Stoughton 1966.

The Practice of the Presence of God, Brother Lawrence. A.R. Mowbray 1923.

God of a Hundred Names, Barbara Greene and Victor Gollancz. Gollancz 1962.

Oxford Book of Christian Verse, ed. Lord David Cecil. Clarendon Press 1965.

Markings, Dag Hammarskjold. Faber 1964.

The Fourth Lesson for the Daily Office, Book One, ed. Christopher Campling. Darton, Longman & Todd 1973.

The Fourth Lesson for the Daily Office, Book Two, ed. Christopher Campling. Darton, Longman & Todd 1974.

Love Is My Meaning: An Anthology of Reassurance, ed. Elizabeth Basset. Darton, Longman & Todd 1973.

Wrestling With Christ, Luigi Santucci. Collins 1972.

A Joy Forever, Patience Strong. A.R. Mowbray 1973.

Pause For Thought on Radio 2. B.B.C. Publications 1971.

Thought For The Day from Radio 4, B.B.C. Publications 1974

The God Who Comes, Carlo Carretto. Darton, Longman & Todd 1974.

In Search Of The Beyond, Carlo Carretto. Darton, Longman & Todd 1975.

Through The Year With William Barclay: Devotional Readings For Every Day, ed. D. Duncan. Hodder & Stoughton 1971.

Every Day With William Barclay, ed. D. Duncan. Hodder & Stoughton 1973.

Through The Year With J.B. Phillips ed. D. Duncan. Hodder & Stoughton 1974.

Through The Year With Michael Ramsay, ed. Margaret Duggon. Hodder & Stoughton 1975.

Give Us . . . The Quiet Mind, Isobel and William Burnett. Mitre Press 1974.

Breaking Through To God, Ladislaus Boros. Darton, Longman & Todd 1973.

The Word Is The Seed, George Appleton. S.P.C.K. 1976.

The Power And Meaning Of Love, Thomas Merton. Sheldon Press 1976.

The Garden Of The Beloved, Robert Way. Sheldon Press 1975.

Readings For Children

Readings Chosen and edited by Denys Thompson. Cambridge University Press 1974.

Words To Share: An Anthology of Poetry and Prose for Use in Christian Education and Worship, Donald H. Hilton. Denholm House Press 1974.

King Of Kings, Malcolm Saville. Lion Publishing 1975.

Here Are Your Saints, Joan Windham. Sheed & Ward 1971. (And others in the same series.)

Donkey's Glory, Nan Goodall. A.R. Mowbray 1974.

Prayers For Children And Young People: An Anthology, Nancy Martin. Hodder & Stoughton 1975.

The Still Small Voice, Johanna Klink. S.C.M. 1974.

Prayers For Children, General Synod Board of Education. C.I.O. 1973.

The Beasts' Choir, Carmen Bernos de Gasztold. (A companion to *Prayers From the Ark*.) Macmillan 1967.

The Ladybird Book of Prayers Through The Year. Ladybird Books 1964.

SOURCES OF PRAYERS

Epigraph (p.xii) from *The Shade of His Hand*, Michael Hollings and Etta Gullick. Mayhew-McCrimmon 1973.

1 Benjamin Jenks in *The One Who Listens*, Michael Hollings and Etta Gullick. Mayhew-McCrimmon 1971.

2 William Bright in *The One Who Listens* (*see* 1).

3 *Draw Near*, Margaret Cropper. S.P.C.K. 1935.

4 *The Sanctuary*, Percy Dearmer. Rivingtons 1930.

5 Source unknown.

6 *A Collection of Prayers for Use in Hospitals*, Colonel Pearson of Bramcote. Derry & Sons 1951.

7 *Private Devotions for the Young in Spirit of All Ages*, Presbyter Anglicanus. S.P.C.K. 1952.

8 Guild of St Raphael.

9 As 8.

10 Source unknown.

11 As 6.

12 *A Book of Prayers for Everyman*. S.P.C.K. 1950.

13 *Prayers New and Old.* Lutterworth Press and Forward Movement Publications 1967.

14 *St Hugh's Prayer Book*. 1929.

15 *A St Francis Prayer Book*, Malcolm L. Playfoot. S.P.C.K. 1967 (adapted).

16 *The Priest to the Altar*, P.G. Medd. Longmans 1898.

17 As 14.

18 As 12.

19 The Order of Confirmation, Book of Common Prayer.

20 Leonine Sacramentary.

21 Gelasian Sacramentary.

22 Post-communion Collect, B.C.P.

23 As 12 (Ps. 150 adapted).

24 Baptismal Service, Church in Wales. Church in Wales Publications.

25 *The Prayer Manual*, F.B. Macnutt. A.R. Mowbray 1961.

26 Baptism and Confirmation, *Alternative Services, Second Series*. C.U.P., Eyre & Spottiswoode, O.U.P., and S.P.C.K. 1968.

27 As 26.

28 *Parish Prayers*, ed. Frank Colquhoun. Hodder & Stoughton 1967.

29 As 26.

30 As 26.

31 As 26.

32 The Prayer Book as proposed in 1928.

33 As 24.

34 As 26.

35 *Comfort and Sure Confidence*, Arthur W. Hopkinson. A.R. Mowbray 1927.

36 William Temple in *The One Who Listens* (*see* 1).

37 *The Priest's Book of Private Devotion*, compiled J. Oldknow and A.D. Crake, revised J.F. Briscoe. A.R. Mowbray 1940.

38 Collect, B.C.P.

39 B.C.P.

40 B.C.P.

41 B.C.P.

42 *Daily Prayer*, ed. Eric Milner-White and G.W. Briggs. O.U.P. 1961.

43 As 35.

44 As 37.

45 As 35.

46 As 37.

47 Scottish Prayer Book.

48 As 47.

49 *Prayers for Christian Healing*, A.E. Campion. A.R. Mowbray 1959.

50 John W. Suter in *The Shade of His Hand*, Michael Hollings and

Etta Gullick. Mayhew McCrimmon 1973.
51 *Daily Prayer and Praise*, George Appleton. World Christian Books, Lutterworth Press 1966.
52 *The Shade of His Hand* (*see* 50).
53 As 49.
54 As 49.
55 Collect for St Luke's Day, American Prayer Book (adapted).
56 As 25.
57 *More Prayers for the Plain Man*, William Barclay. Collins Fontana 1962.
58 *Worship in the Young Wives' Group*, Jean Yeomans. Epworth Press 1966.
59 As 42.
60 Compiler.
61 *A Diocesan Service Book*, ed. L.S. Hunter. O.U.P. 1965.
62 *Prayers for All Occasions.* Lutterworth Press and Forward Movement Publications 1964 (adapted).
63 Prayer for 'Universities and Colleges', used in King's College, Cambridge (adapted).
64 S.P.T. Prideaux, No. 1172 in *Parish Prayers* (*see* 28).
65 As 28 (adapted).
66 As 42.
67 Compiler.
68 Compiler.
69 Alfred Torrie in *Prayers for Christian Healing* (see 49).
70 As 6.
71 As 8.
72 *New Every Morning*, (rev. edn). BBC Publications 1973.
73 As 25.
74 *Prayers for Help and Healing*, William Barclay. Collins Fontana 1968 (adapted).
75 Source unknown.
76 *A Little Book of Devotion for Nurses*, Doreen Pearce. A.R. Mowbray 1948.
77 As 28.
78 *Sursum Corda.* A.R. Mowbray 1898.
79 As 78.
80 As 72.
81 As 15 (adapted).
82 Compiler.
83 As 74 (adapted).
84 As 6 (adapted).
85 As 13.
86 As 74 (adapted).
87 As 62.
88 As 62.
89 A.F. Leatherland, No. 1445 in *Parish Prayers* (*see* 28) (adapted).
90 As 74 (adapted).
91 As 28.
92 Compiler.
93 Compiler.
94 Compiler.
95 As 13.
96 As 72.
97 As 25.
98 Source unknown.
99 As 74 (adapted).
100 Canadian Prayer Book (adapted).
101 Compiler.
102 *The Shade of His Hand* (*see* 50).
103 *Epilogues and Prayers*, William Barclay. S.C.M. Press 1963.
104 *Jerusalem Prayers for the World Today*, George Appleton. S.P.C.K. 1974.
105 As 61 (adapted).
106 As 51.
107 S.P.G. Prayer Card: 'Medical Missions', compiled by George Appleton.
108 *Prayers for Today's Church*, ed. Dick Williams. C.P.A.S. Publications 1972.
109 As 47.
110 As 62.
111 As 6.

112 As 51.
113 E.B. Pusey.
114 As 25.
115 *A Chain of Prayer Across the Ages*, ed. S.F. Fox. John Murray 1956.
116 As 25.
117 *It's Me, O Lord*, Michael Hollings and Etta Gullick. Mayhew-McCrimmon 1972.
118 *The Shade of His Hand* (*see* 50).
119 As 15.
120 Irish Prayer Book.
121 As 15.
122 *For Your Comfort*. Churches' Council for Health and Healing.
123 As 76.
124 As 108.
125 As 61.
126 As 32.
127 As 13.
128 As 108.
129 As 62.
130 As 13.
131 Eric Milner-White in *The Shade of His Hand* (*see* 50).
132 As 13.
133 As 13.
134 As 107.
135 As 113.
136 *The Shade of His Hand* (*see* 50).
137 *Prayers of Motherhood*. Mothers' Union.
138 As 108.
139 As 137.
140 Guild of Health.
141 As 13.
142 As 120.
143 *A Hospital Prayer Book* (4th edn). O.U.P. 1954.
144 As 107.
145 As 143 (adapted).
146 As 74 (adapted).
147 'The Covenant of Peace' in *The Shade of His Hand* (*see* 50).
148 *The Priest's Vade Mecum*. S.P.C.K. 1945 (adapted).
149 As 108.
150 *Prayers for Today*, edited and compiled by Norman W. Goodacre. A.R. Mowbray 1973.
151 As 62.
152 As 150.
153 As 72.
154 As 72.
155 As 150.
156 As 120.
157 As 28.
158 *A Diary of Prayer*, Elizabeth Goudge. Hodder & Stoughton 1966.
159 As 51.
160 Compiler.
161 *An Anthology of Prayers*, A.S.T. Fisher. Longmans 1950.
162 *Words for Worship*, C.R. Campling and M. Davis. Edward Arnold 1969.
163 As 25.
164 As 150.
165 As 51.
166 Compiler.
167 Richard Meux Benson in *The One Who Listens* (*see* 1).
168 Margaret Dewey in *New Every Morning* (*see* 72).
169 As 108.
170 As 15.
171 As 15.
172 Source unknown.
173 As 13.
174 As 62.
175 As 8.
176 As 72.
177 As 13.
178 *Prayers Old and New*, A.W. Robinson. S.C.M. Press 1932.
179 As 49.
180 As 8.
181 As 51.
182 As 15.
183 As 115.

184 As 115.
185 *Handmaids of the Sick.* Faith Press 1929.
186 Anonymous, quoted in *The One Who Listens* (*see* 1).
187 As 15.
188 As 72.
189 As 120 (adapted).
190 As 49.
191 Phoebe Hesketh in *New Every Morning* (*see* 72).
192 As 72.
193 As 72.
194 As 62.
195 As 51.
196 *The One Who Listens* (*see* 1).
197 Anonymous, quoted in *The Shade of His Hand* (*see* 50).
198 William Temple.
199 John Wordsworth in the *Salisbury Book of Occasional Offices* 1917.
200 As 25.
201 East Syrian Daily Office, quoted in *The Shade of His Hand* (*see* 50).
202 As 100 (adapted).
203 *The Shade of His Hand* (*see* 50).
204 *The One Who Listens* (*see* 1).
205 As 72.
206 *The Shade of His Hand* (*see* 50).
207 As 100 (adapted).
208 As 120.
209 *Prayers at Breakfast*, Beryl Bye. Lutterworth Press 1964.
210 As 42.
211 *The Shade of His Hand* (*see* 50).
212 William Bright.
213 As 42.
214 Acts. 7.55-6.
215 As 113.
216 *Prayers of Comfort for the Sorrowing.* Mothers' Union.
217 *Acts of Devotion* (old edn). S.P.C.K. 1954.
218 As 115.
219 Compiler.
220 *A Form of Thanksgiving to Almighty God after Serious Illness.* S.P.C.K. 1958.
221 As 42.
222)
to)As 72.
244)
245)
to)As 13.
250)
251 Ps.72.18-19.
252 Ps.121.8.
253 Dan.2.20.
254 Tobit 13.1.
255 Rev.1.5,6.
256 Rev.5.13.

Prayers 251 to 256 are adapted from the more familiar versions of the Psalms and the Bible.

INDEX